TREASURES OF THE WORDSWORTH TRUST

ROBERT WOOF

Treasures of the Wordsworth Trust

Published to celebrate the opening of

THE JERWOOD CENTRE
AT THE WORDSWORTH TRUST

by Seamus Heaney

2 June 2005

THE WORDSWORTH TRUST

GRASMERE

Published by the Wordsworth Trust
Dove Cottage, Grasmere, Cumbria LA22 9SH
© 2005 All rights reserved

ISBN 1 905256 00 0

Designed by Stephen Hebron
Photography by Alex Black
Set in Monotype Dante
Printed by Titus Wilson, Kendal

TO JONATHAN WORDSWORTH

who was there

PREFACE

Treasures of the Wordsworth Trust has been published to celebrate the opening of the Jerwood Centre by Seamus Heaney on 2 June 2005. It gives a selection of one hundred items from the Trust's collections of books, manuscripts, paintings, drawings and engravings that have been built up since the Trust's foundation in 1891.

The Trustees are very grateful to Val and Tony Mortlock, the Michael Marks Trust, the Northern Rock Foundation, Rural Regeneration Cumbria, and the European Regional Development Fund for supporting this publication and exhibition.

My long-term thanks are to the Trustees who, in my personal experience over thirty-five years, have supported in every ingenious way the building of these collections.

And for the production of this catalogue, my especial thanks go first to Stephen Hebron, who has masterminded its structure, the selection of objects, and the quality of the design. I am extremely grateful to Sally Woodhead for, once again, accepting the challenge of having to create a finished text in a remarkably short period. Hamish Robinson gave to my essay valuable and elegant turns of style; and Richard Stanton made very valuable suggestions. Jeff Cowton gleaned our records for facts, and there was real joy in discovering so much. We became conscious that there are hundreds of small donations to the Trust's collections which are recorded, but to which it is impossible to do justice in this one selection. My greatest debt, throughout the writing of this catalogue, and in everything, is to Pamela Woof, with whom I am always in dialogue, and who is always illuminating.

CONTENTS

The Founding of the Wordsworth Trust and the Building of its Collections

FROM THE VERY beginning, in 1891, the Wordsworth Trust was committed to building a collection, but admittedly this was the Trust's second rather than its first purpose: the first being the acquisition of Dove Cottage as a living memorial to Wordsworth and his poetry. The first Trustees were conscious that Dove Cottage was the third such shrine in England: Shakespeare's birthplace had been opened to the public in the 1840s; Milton's cottage at Chalfont St Giles in the 1870s; and so in 1890, Wordsworth's cottage was purchased for £650 from Edmund Lee, a Bradford enthusiast (and later a Trustee) who had published *Dorothy Wordsworth: The Story of a Sister's Love*, in 1886. The Cottage was acquired by a group of Englishmen led by a former Royal Chaplain, Stopford Brooke (1832–1916). Brooke had left the Church of England in 1880, unable to accept the miracle of the Incarnation and the Church's conservative politics. He had delighted Queen Victoria, but her wish to make him a Canon of Westminster was opposed: Disraeli disliked Brooke's Christian Socialist politics (Bernard Shaw made him the model for the Reverend James Morell in *Candida*, in 1893) and Gladstone was suspicious of his theology ('very noteworthy, a little perilous', he noted in his diary). Without becoming a Unitarian, Brooke preached mainly in Unitarian churches. He was an admirable intellectual figure, literary to the core, and a personal friend of both Tennyson and Browning (he wrote a book on each of them), capable of writing a history of English literature from the Anglo-Saxon to the contemporary scene. Brooke had Irish origins, and there are fascinating glimpses in his diary of the young W.B. Yeats, whom he met while visiting his mother in Dublin:

> … I met Yeats swaying about in Dawson St. His body & his hair were equally long. His speech strayed like his hair. His thinness, & he is tall & willowy, suits him, and so do his dark eyes. He said he would dine with me, but Miss Gonne is about some where & he may fly with her. Why he is involved with that loud-cackling goose, I cannot tell. But I have never seen her, & she may be seductive. A poet ought to marry – if he marries – a gentle, steady, good woman, who will confess him

to be a poet, admire him, but keep him in order, & in harmony with the Earth & Man. Flighty things don't suit, or ideal creatures, or the harlot type. They overstimulate, & the man, having soared beyond himself, his wings are melted, & he drops down like Icarus. Just think of Alfred de Musset! Mrs Browning, who *was* ideal, was also full of the common sense of home.

But there is, among many texts (and these wonderful diaries were given by Peter and Henry Brooke on behalf of the Brooke family), one other to bear in mind, and that is Stopford Brooke's inaugural address to the Shelley Society in 1886. He makes it his business here to reply to Matthew Arnold's dismissal of Shelley as 'an ineffectual angel' at the end of Arnold's essay on Byron. Stopford Brooke was challenging:

> Were society to alter, as it must soon alter or disintegrate, away from this condition, and live more in the hopes, and with the aims, and in the simple life, of Shelley, and along with these also possess his sanity of view, it would then understand how foolish it is to call him 'a beautiful but ineffectual angel, beating in the void his luminous wings in vain.' Towards that change, his work in poetry concerning man is one element of power; but I fear those that move too far apart from the more ideal hopes of man, in the midst of a formulated culture, will not see or understand that this is true. … If you wish to be in the forefront of the future, if you wish to live in the ideas which will, thirty years hence, rule the world, live among the men who are indignant and who hope with Shelley, who have his faith, who hear the trumpet of a prophecy and whose cry day and night is this –
> O wind,
> If winter comes, can spring be far behind …

It was this idealist ardour in Stopford Brooke which gave him a visionary touch; certainly it influenced what Dove Cottage was to become: it was to be, in Brooke's own phrase, 'for the eternal possession of those who love English poetry from all over the world' (Stopford Brooke, *Dove Cottage*, 1892, 14). Brooke had the sensitivity and the scholarship to have a lively and personal view of the continuing relevance of the Romantic writers, especially the poets. When he first read *The Prelude* as a young man, he wrote on the title-page, amending Wordsworth's subtitle, 'An Autobiographical poem', with a rare and mischievous word. He called it 'An Autoleilistical poem', a poem, that is, devoted too exclusively to worshipping the self. In this flash of wit Brooke shows how surprised people were by Wordsworth's egotistical concerns in *The Prelude* when the poem was first published in 1850. However, the poem was later much re-read by Brooke, as his well-worn copy attests. It was not until the 1926 edition of the 1805 text of *The Prelude,* the work of Brooke's successor as Chairman of the Trust, Ernest de Selincourt, was it possible to understand how original Wordsworth's autobiography was (in its language, its theology, its psychological probing) when it was first written at the beginning of the nineteenth century.

But more of Stopford Brooke's lively spirit emerges from his diary: it is clear that he was able to get things started at Grasmere. He was fortunate to have his lawyer brother William as his principal ally; and he managed to make some useful, if sometimes overbearing, Trustees work together. Canon Rawnsley (who was, with others, to found the National Trust in 1895) emerges as someone inclined to insist on his own importance. An almost comic moment comes when Brooke reports the insertion of a memorial stone to John Wordsworth among the Wordsworth family graves at Grasmere. Wordsworth himself had not wanted there to be any explanation of who he was, requiring simply names and death-dates, and this minimalism the family had respected. But the Trustees by 1904 decided, not inappropriately, to add a memorial to Wordsworth's brother John Wordsworth (1772–1805), who had drowned almost a century before, on 5 February 1805, as Commander of one of the finest East Indiamen, *The Earl of Abergavenny*, which sand with the loss of almost 400 lives. Brooke's diary records the touches of gentle animosity that surrounded their good deed:

> I visited the Churchyard & saw the Stone Rawnsley & I got put up to John Wordsworth between that of William & of Dorothy. I am glad to have done that. It was characteristic of Rawnsley when I spoke to him about it last year that he said he had always wished it & suggested it. The fact is he had never thought of it till I suggested it to him some years ago. I said nothing. If he wishes to have his fingers in every pie, he may always be first for all I care. What I wanted was to have the thing done. He may keep all the credit of it if he likes. But I don't think he really desires that. William [Brooke] & [George Lillie] Craik subscribed four pounds to it. Rawnsley & I six.

Stopford Brooke outside Dove Cottage

The stones read as follows:

> To the memory of / JOHN WORDSWORTH brother of William and Dorothy / A Silent Poet and cherished Visitant and Lover of this valley / Born 4 December 1772. He died at his post as Commander / of the Earl of Abergavenny which / was wrecked in the English Channel / 5 February 1805. He was buried at / Wyke Regis

Not insignificantly, after two centuries (and much research), this tragic episode led to the Trustees organising (with the help of Patrick Tolfree), on 13 April 2005, the erection of a memorial – dedicated by the Bishop of Salisbury – in Wyke Regis Church in the presence of the Wordsworth family and their friends.

But what comes across from the diary is that Brooke took particular pleasure in the garden of Dove Cottage. It is no wonder that there are such delightful photographs of him, either standing in his cloak in the garden or sitting comfortably by the back-stair doorway created by Catherine and Thomas Clarkson in 1804:

William Knight by Maud Coleman, 1890

I went to see Dove Cottage this morning with Mr. New, & took over his drawings of the place. The garden looked charming. All the rhododendrons are in full flower, & make the grass & grey walls bright with lovely colour. The Osmunda Fern by the rock-pool is stately. It may well be called Regalis. The trees in the orchard are thick with apple-knobs. As to the grass, it is smooth, softer than sleep, of a lovely green.

Edmund Hart New's drawings, incidentally, are still within the Trust's collections.

Brooke then goes on to talk about the 'Museum Room': 'The new arrangements in the Museum Room are most satisfactory: & all the pictures are hung'. The Museum Room had become necessary because of the strong views of William Knight, the Professor of Moral Philosophy at St Andrew's. He had been the first secretary of the Wordsworth Society, from 1880 to 1886, and, arguably, the first scholarly editor of Wordsworth's poems and the first independent biographer of the poet. He was the first to present some of the textual variants from the manuscripts in his eleven-volume edition of

1882–9; and he included generous extracts from the manuscripts of Dorothy Wordsworth's Journals, written at Alfoxden and at Grasmere. The original Trust deed of 1 December 1891 had specified that, if there were any money to spare after the purchase of the Cottage, it should be devoted to founding a Library. After more than a dozen years of inaction, Knight felt the Trustees had not fulfilled their duty and, leading by example, he gave a fine collection of Wordsworth first editions, all bound in leather or leatherette. It was this primary gift of books, along with photographs and manuscripts, that persuaded the Trustees to make a formal museum in the room that had been added to Dove Cottage by Levi Hodgson, then living at How Top Farm, in 1849. The arrangements for the new museum room were put in the hands of Professor Armstrong at a meeting on 6 June 1899 (in London): 'We gave Armstrong full powers. I hope he won't make the thing a failure. Knight did not turn up to Craik's surprise, not to mine'. Armstrong lived in Edinburgh and there are copies of Wordsworth's *Poems* given by Brooke to Armstrong: what did surprise Brooke was that Armstrong should come to hear his lecture in Edinburgh on 26 November 1899:

> Armstrong came to see us. I was astonished to see him, for he wrote a very rude letter to Craik about me & Dove Cottage. He was as big & bluff as ever – a man-mountain. I wonder of what steel or special wood his bedstead is made! It must have learned creaking by this time.

It looks as if Armstrong made a decent job of the first museum room. Indeed, when Armstrong died in 1900, the Trustees recorded that his 'interest in Dove Cottage was unceasing, his visits to it and his care for it continuous.'

But Rawnsley was a more difficult figure. In a letter to Gordon Wordsworth (1863–1935), Beatrix Potter made it clear that Canon Rawnsley was not her favourite person. Describing a prized 'old ledger' which had been discovered in one of her properties – the ledger formerly had belonged to Ann Tyson and contained the accounts covering Wordsworth's time as her lodger – she makes it plain that it is for the eyes of Gordon Wordsworth alone:

> Only – if I lend it to you for your own litterary [sic] use – may I make two conditions? – That eventually I am at liberty to hand the ledger to Hawkshead Grammar school – and secondly that you will not without my consent hand it to any other bookmaker? I especially bar Canon

Canon Hardwicke Rawnsley (1851–1920)

Rawnsley! Where Willie [her husband, William Heelis] seems to have informed you that the book is a secret; that is all a mystery. I dispute that the Canon has any exclusive property in the Poet; and knowing my own slowness and his certain inquisitiveness – I didn't want him to get wind of it – (and I don't still! to tell the truth).

Brooke found Canon Rawnsley's attitude to clean linen difficult to bear:

We met R[awnsley], with a frayed & buttonless shirt on, & dirty cuffs. It doesn't matter in the Country, any more than in a studio what sort of coat you wear …

But Rawnsley was also one of the considerable amateur scholars who made the subject of Wordsworth and his relation to the Lake District terrain a continuing field of research. Stephen Gill has remarked that Rawnsley's address to the Wordsworth Society in 1883 clearly expressed three major ideas: first, that 'England is beginning to become a nation that believes in education … At least the vales of Cumberland and Westmorland, charged with the spirit of Wordsworth, must be left ... as Nature's own English university in the age of great cities'. The notion that the Lake District was 'not only *pleasure* grounds but *thinking* grounds, & capable only of enriching the nation with high thoughts & so are part of the nation's wealth' was the high ground that was the basis of his second notion that the Lake District should have a defence society. And the third idea was that there should be a national park (as had been devised in the USA with the acquisition of Yosemite Valley). Of course, the immediate result of Rawnsley's gifted campaign was, with Octavia Hill, the foundation of the National Trust on 12 January 1895. This public sympathy for the preservation of the Lake District was never part of the Wordsworth Trust's actual agenda, but its Trustees were sympathetically linked.

The appointments to the Trustees continued to exhibit the same mixture of practical and scholarly eminence. In 1904 Ernest Hartley Coleridge, the greatest of Coleridge editors since the poet's death, was appointed and, in 1907, joined by Ernest de Selincourt, perhaps the most important Wordsworth scholar of the twentieth century. Another appointment was G.M. Trevelyan, later Master of Trinity College, Cambridge, raised the national profile of the Trust. He was joined by an equally significant figure, Wordsworth's grandson Gordon Wordsworth. Three years before his election, Gordon Wordsworth had proposed entrusting the Wordsworth MSS to the care of the Trustees. Twenty-one years later, in 1935, this important and wonderful bequest changed the Trust into a major academic centre. The papers themselves comprised 90% of Wordsworth's working notebooks and a major part of the family correspondence; they were also wonderfully rich in letters written to the Wordsworths by major figures of their time. Dora Wordsworth's autograph book gives some sense of the range of correspondence. Tennyson said there was no crime that an autograph hunter would not commit, but Dora did not have to be very wicked: her collection is a cultural audit of those whom the Wordsworths knew. The first letter is from Lord Nelson to Sir Alexander Ball, the first British Governor of Malta, and had clearly been scooped up by Coleridge when he was Ball's secretary in 1804. The second is a holograph letter from George Washington to Arthur Lee, congratulating him in 1785 for his skill in negotiating treaties with the western tribes of the Indians. Its origin in Dora's collection is not clear, but the significance is: Washington was a hero to the Wordsworths, as to many Englishmen. The letter from an English hero, Charles James Fox, in answer to Wordsworth's great letter of January 1801 (where he states the purpose

Gordon Graham Wordsworth (1863–1935)

of his writing was to show that 'men who do not wear fine cloathes can feel deeply') is both courteous and frank:

> I read with particular attention the two you pointed out ['The Brothers' and 'Michael'], but whether it be from my early prepossessions, or whatever other cause, I am no great friend to blank verse subjects which are to be treated of with simplicity. You will excuse my stating to you my opinion so freely, which I should not do if I did not really admire many of the poems in the collection, and many parts even of these in blank verse.

Dora had over 170 letters, including those of writers such as Walter Scott and William Wilberforce. She even included one from Thomas De Quincey. This autograph book is only the first of several great autograph collections which the Trust now owns.

Until that great gift came from Gordon Wordsworth, much of the Trustees' business was to see that the properties were open to a general public and were maintained at a good standard. The staff was originally small, Mrs Mary Dixon and her daughter; but later, by and until the 1970s, the permanent staff expanded to four. The Trustees quietly strengthened their preservation of the hamlet of Town End by purchasing properties. These developments were in the hands of a local committee to which, in 1915, W.A. Spooner, the Warden of New College, was added. As his wife was the daughter of Harvey Goodwin, the Bishop of Carlisle, and as Goodwin's daughters jointly owned How Foot, he lived in How Foot, which then held the garden across the road adjoining Dove Cottage. It was a prudent scheme that allowed the Spooners to sell part of the garden to the Trustees to protect the southern boundary of Dove Cottage. The five Sykeside cottages were bought in 1930. Now, in 2005, the Trust owns twenty-three small properties, and these acquisitions have made it possible to house thirty members of staff on the site. Without this forethought about housing, the effective operation of the Trust in its present form would be impossible.

The Trustees in 1915 discussed whether women could be admitted to their ranks. It was not until 1919 that Evelyn Brooke was elected. Eleanor Rawnsley, the second wife of the Canon, followed, and dominated Grasmere life for nearly forty years from her home at Allan Bank. Helen Darbishire (later Head of Somerville College), a close academic colleague of Ernest de Selincourt, ultimately became Chairman. There were few elections until 1933, when Lascelles Abercrombie, Vita Sackville-West (Mrs Harold Nicolson), Edith Batho and Henry Brooke, the future Home Secretary, all came to the Trust. Key figures elected during the Second World War were Joanna Hutchinson and Dorothy Dickson; they were respectively the heirs to the great manuscript collections of the Hutchinson family and the Wordsworth family, and they subsequently and generously bequeathed the greater part of their collections to the Trust. The Trustees were fortunate in their academic strength, in their support from the Wordsworth family, and in the support of the families of the first Trustees; and they were also lucky in being able to gather in freelance scholars such as E.P. Thompson and Simon Nowell-Smith. Scholarly mountaineers, such as Peter Bicknell, Charles Warren (the doctor on two Everest expeditions in the 1930s) and Oliver Turnbull, brought a renewed interest in the quality of the Trust's book-collecting: Peter Bicknell's is still the standard bibliography of books of the English Lake District. It is perhaps appropriate to list those who have been Chairmen of the Trust: their guidance has been crucial throughout: Rev. Stopford Brooke (1891–1916); Canon H.D. Rawnsley (1918–1919); Professor Ernest de Selincourt (1920–1942); Miss Helen Darbishire (1944–1960); Professor Basil Willey (1961–1972); Dr Mary Moorman (1973–1976); Professor Jonathan Wordsworth (1977–2002); the Rt Hon Chris Smith (2002–present).

The collections at Dove Cottage were 'Designated' in 1997 as a collection of national and international importance. There are some 30,000 manuscripts, 12,000 books and 8,000 prints, drawings and paintings. At first, the collection grew slowly. After William Knight's gifts of books and manuscripts, new items came as single spies rather than in battalions. In 1914, Mr Joel Cadbury offered the Trustees letters written by Thomas Clarkson, in which he described the details of the death of Charles Gough, the young Quaker who had fallen from Striding Edge on 17 April 1805: he had been found three months later with his dog still beside him. Scott and Wordsworth both wrote poems about the fidelity of the dog, which led to many drawings, paintings and scultures on the same theme. By 2002, the Trust had such an accumulation of documents and works of art that it was able to mount an exhibition on this theme alone: *The Unfortunate Tourist of Helvellyn and his faithful dog*.

From these small beginnings, the Trustees have gone on to accumulate material relating to Wordsworth's circle; and that circle is truly large, containing over 3,000 writers and artists. The importance of Wordsworth as a major (and controversial) writer in his time is not always recognised. In our collection, the dominant presence of William and Dorothy Wordsworth is only to be expected; as is that of figures such as Coleridge, Southey and De Quincey; but it is the sheer range of cultural interconnections within the collection that provides an unexpected opportunity for studying and interpreting a major period in the history of this country and, indeed, of the western world.

The Trust has found itself undertaking an exhibition on great themes: the Age of Revolutions, the Discovery of Nature, the new emphasis upon the human mind – memory, the imagination and the sublime. All these themes are reflected in a collection which include not just the books and writings of individual authors, but every conceivable kind of material recording the interaction between writers, fine artists and leading thinkers of the time. Hence, the Trust has acquired not only portraits of the leading Romantic figures, but also landscape paintings, particularly of the Lake District. One must remember that at least three hundred writers, including John Stuart Mill, Matthew Arnold and John Ruskin, made significant comment on Wordsworth's writings in his own lifetime, so the cultural debate was huge.

It would have been naive to exclude from our concern for Romantic literature those who are not especially connected with Grasmere – Blake, Shelley, Byron, Keats, Mary Wollstonecraft, Jane Austen and Mary Shelley. Equally, it has become increasingly clear that the Northern Renaissance stretched across the border and embraced the work of Burns and Scott. As De Quincey found, it was as easy to go to Edinburgh from Grasmere as to London. The American exhibition, *William Wordsworth and the Age of English Romanticism* (with catalogue by Jonathan Wordsworth, Michael C. Jaye and Robert Woof), in 1987, brought out the importance of a cultural moment in British history that embraced a world of revolutions, from the American to the French, the study of the place of nature in the minds of the great Romantics, and the parallel theme of response to landscape of major artists such as Gainsborough, Towne, Wright of Derby, Turner, Cotman, Constable, Cox, Girtin, John and Cornelius Varley, and De Wint. In 1981, the Trust had only one major English watercolour, a drawing of Grasmere by John White Abbott (which is on the front cover of this book). Since then some fifty artists have been added to the collection, though, to be precise, some are, as yet, only promised as bequests at a future time. No-one could have expected works by Edward Dayes, Joseph Farington, John Bernard Gilpin, William Gilpin, John Laporte, Lady Mary Lowther, Edward Lear, Francis Nicholson, Richard Ramsay Reinagle, William Havell, George Fennell Robson, John 'Warwick' Smith, Thomas Sunderland, Francis Towne, John Constable, J.M.W. Turner and Joseph Wilkinson to have formed part of our rich harvest. It is sometimes said by scholars that no major landscape artists has painted the Lake District; this is clearly an exaggerated and pessimistic view. More importantly, most of the artists working in the Lake District (as is true of artists of every age) were in close contact with the writers of their time. Increasingly, the Trust's work has been to ferret out evidence of the cross-disciplinary influence of poets and painters. A typical discovery came when the Trust acquired, 1988, the letters of William Cookson, Wordsworth's uncle. In a letter to his fiancée, 1783, Cookson noted that he had been providing descriptive text for the letterpress accompanying Farington's prints of the Lake District (the text, in French and English, was printed anonymously):

> I am to dine with Farington tomorrow. I have been employed for a sort of *Authorship* for him, viz. a brief Description of each of his Views, which will be published about Christmas. As I am but little satisfied with my performance keep this to yourself.

Once it is understood that Farington and Wordsworth's uncle were close friends, it becomes clear that Wordsworth was brought up in a household that had an interest in drawings. In another recently acquired document, Amelia Opie's conversation with George Richmond, December 1836, records:

> That Opie said of Wordsworth that he talked on art more sensibly and more like an artist than anybody he had met not in the profession.

Since Opie died in 1807, we are clearly dealing with Wordsworth at the height of his literary powers. Wordsworth was a writer who liked artists. 'O now that the genius of Bewick were mine / And the skill which he learned on the banks of the Tyne', he wrote in 1800: not surprisingly, the collecting of Bewick's work is of major interest to the Trust.

The Trust owns some of the great portraits of Wordsworth; the Trust was fortunate that the Fisher-Wordsworths left them the head-and-shoulders portrait by Pickersgill as early as the 1920s; Joanna Hutchinson left the Richard Carruthers portrait (1818) upon her death; and Eleanor Rawnsley left the Edridge portrait (1805) in 1959. The Trustees' relationship with the National Portrait Gallery and the Scottish National Portrait Galley has allowed us to have on long-term loan major portraits of Walter Scott, Lord Byron, John Wilson, Humphry Davy, Benjamin Robert Haydon, William Godwin, Leigh Hunt and Charles and Mary Lamb. The posthumous portrait of Shelley at the Baths of Caracalla has been lent by Lord Abinger. But to those holdings, the Trustees have been able to add major portraits of Southey, Coleridge, Hartley Coleridge, Sara Coleridge, and splendid life-masks of Wordsworth and Keats (both by Haydon) and one of Coleridge (on generous long-term loan). The life-mask is an indication of the near photographic methods of portrayal that artists drew upon when preparing a portrait. Just before the opening of this exhibition, the Trust acquired a portrait of Thomas De Quincey with his three daughters and grandchild by James Archer from De Quincey's own family, now living in Holland. No doubt many important opportunities yet remain.

It is worth remembering that the early Trustees could have blind spots. When I first came as a student to the Wordsworth Library (in the downstairs of the present shop), I was visited by Eleanor Rawnsley, who asked me what I was reading. I confessed to reading De Quincey's *Recollections of the Lake Poets*. Her answer was severe: 'De Quincey tells lies. You should read Ernest de Selincourt on Dorothy Wordsworth, where all is truth.' It was not until the exhibition of 1985 that the Trustees seriously began to accumulate editions of the 'untruthful' De Quincey; it was not until 1989 that the Trustees took the decision to purchase the manuscript of *The Confessions of an English Opium-Eater*. This led to the formation of an editorial team under Professor Grevel Lindop and the publication, completed 2003, of a twenty-one volume new edition of De Quincey's works (published by Pickering & Chatto). It is precisely such scholarship that has prompted the Trustees to acquire collections. Over two hundred De Quincey manuscripts were purchased to assist the editorial team.

Perhaps the Trust's most astonishing acquisition came in 1977: the intimate letters of the poet and his wife, Mary (née Hutchinson). They revealed a more passionate Wordsworth than biographers, up to that point, had discovered, although in the manuscript of his *Table-Talk*, Coleridge had noted that he considered Wordsworth to be much more passionate in all matters than himself. The new letters are not only fine in themselves, but they also reveal a strength and equal power in his wife Mary.

Wordsworth always loved women, and they appreciated him. It has become an increasing element of our understanding of the Romantic movement to recognise the part Wordsworth played in the changing sensibility of the age. His correspondence shows that, just as his domestic life is centred on the women in his family, so, in his literary appreciation, women were highly significant. His first published poem, a sonnet in *The European Magazine*, 4 February 1787, was dedicated to Helen Maria Williams, the radical writer caught up in the French Revolution; indeed it was to visit Miss Williams that Wordsworth went to Orléans in 1791, to find that she had left for Paris. It was then that he met Annette Vallon who led him back to her home town of Blois, where their love affair led to the birth of a daughter, Caroline. The story of Annette was difficult for the early Trustees; those who knew, it seems, dared not publish it. Gordon Wordsworth had, finally, to accept the fact of Annette's relationship with Wordsworth, which was proved by letters in the French archives relating to the city of Blois (published by Gordon Maclean Harper in 1916); even so, in 1950, when a play was devised in Ambleside to celebrate the author, Joyce Cockcroft was told that she must omit all references to the French affair. And even in 1981, a senior member of the Wordsworth family upbraided me for including Annette and Caroline on the family tree. But out of these debates has come a fuller understanding of Wordsworth. In later years the letters he exchanged with Felicia Hemans and, above all, with Isabella Fenwick, a star in the evening of Wordsworth's life, show that despite living in a masculine world, Wordsworth always reached across the gap in gender.

The secrets of the private lives of poets inevitably emerge. Coleridge's story is richly caught in Dorothy Wordsworth's Journals which have been progressively edited over a century, with new readings still emerging. But Coleridge's verse-letter to Sara Hutchinson, dated 4 April 1802 (but not published until 1937), was to give a much more agonised portrait of Coleridge's mental life. The confessional power of the verse-letter was later reorganised in the more formal structure of 'Dejection: An Ode' (1817); manuscripts, not least the letters of Sara Hutchinson herself, ensure that we do not have a story of total pathos. The papers relating to *The Friend*, a magazine published from Grasmere, 1809-10, depended upon Sara's secretarial work; her own letters are feisty and independent, and give us a good idea of why Coleridge was so devoted.

Nothing can surprise one in the manuscript world. Another unexpected gift was the Shepherd Papers, the Wordsworth family accounts which cover the time when Wordsworth and his brothers were at Hawkshead School. They came from Jane Lightfoot, who originally had married Wordsworth's eldest brother Richard. These accounts were the basis of T.W. Thompson's detailed study, *Wordsworth's Hawkshead*, 1970, of Wordsworth's time with Ann Tyson while a pupil at Hawkshead School (1779–1787). In 1994, the Ingleby-Roberts family, who had emigrated to Canada, came together and, in memory of their mother, presented their papers relating to Richard's son, called 'Keswick John' to distinguish him from many other John Wordsworths – the occasion of a joyous reunion in Grasmere.

Then, in 1982, John Spedding of Mirehouse, Bassenthwaite, who had been a Trustee for over ten years, decided to make a long-term deposit of all his family papers. These not only deal with the Speddings, who were contemporaries of Wordsworth and also went to Hawkshead School, but with a second generation, of whom the most famous is James Spedding, Tennyson's closest friend after Arthur Hallam. These papers are used by all Tennyson scholars; they were the basis of Robert Martin's biography (1980) and were used by Cecil Lang in his edition of Tennyson's letters. The collection led to the Trust's creating one of the largest of their exhibitions in 1992, in celebration of the centenary of Tennyson's death. Since the Speddings were a family with great intellectual interest, this correspondence includes letters from Thomas Carlyle to James Speddings's brother, Thomas Storey Spedding, and a wonderful series of family letters which show how carefully the children of the John Spedding who was Wordsworth's contemporary were nurtured. An exquisite dispute between James and his father over whether James should concern himself with mathematics and get a good Honours degree, or whether he should pursue his literary idol, Wordsworth, and other literary matters, is typical of the riches the papers hold. Another delicious cross-reference came to light with the presentation of half of the Blamire papers by Dr Christopher Maycock, a descendant of the Blamire family, among whom the best known was the poet Susanna Blamire (1747–1794). In writing her biography, he needed to establish a possible link between Byron and Susanna, and discovered that William Brown, whose mother was a Blamire, had first taught Annabella Milbanke, Byron's wife, and then the Spedding family at Mirehouse: clearly, it was possible that Byron in *Childe Harold*, III, and 'The Prisoner of Chillon' had been influenced by one of Susanna's poems. From the presentation of the Blamire Papers, two kindnesses followed. Susan Thornely, on behalf of the Curwen family, deposited the typescript (all that survives) of the eighteenth-century diaries of Jane Blamire, and Professor Paul Betz generously indicated that it was his intention to leave the Trust the Blamire papers that he had purchased from Christopher's mother.

Canon Rawnsley, in his article, 'The Last of the Calverts' *The Cornhill Magazine*, 1890, published a sentence indicating that he had once seen a letter of Raisley Calvert's, the young man who died, aged 21, who had generously arranged that William and Dorothy Wordsworth should receive legacies of £600 and £300 respectively. Clearly, any letter of Calvert's was of interest to the Trust. When the Trust made contact with Raisley Moorsom in 1983, he made it plain that his brother had received the land and he had received the papers, and he felt that some compensation was due. Fortunately, Paul Channon, then Minister of Arts, signed the agreement that allowed Raisley Moorsom to give the Trust the papers in lieu of paying tax. The Moorsom Papers are a veritable cultural index of life in the English Lake District in the nineteenth-century. The 1,200 names in this great autograph collection was put together by Mary Stanger (née Calvert), who was the niece of Raisley and the daughter of his elder brother William, who lived at Windy Brow. The 1,200 names include many national figures from the judiciary, as well as bishops and generals. But there is a concentration of literary figures: Mary had been able to raid the wastepaper baskets of Wordsworth, Coleridge and Southey. One might have hoped that she would have had something of Shelley's, who knew and admired the Calvert family when he stayed in Keswick in 1810–1811. However, Shelley is absent. There are five letters of

John Stuart Mill to Mary's brother, William, who was also a close friend of John Sterling. Sterling and Calvert are the two young men who feature to prominently in Caroline Fox's journals – both men were dying of tuberculosis at Falmouth – and it seems that they were much loved by Caroline and her sister. Justice is not easily done to such a miscellaneous collection: there are magnificent letters, such as that from David Livingstone on the discovery of Victoria Falls; but also other letters between Wordsworth and the Calverts and, most interestingly, the letter from Raisley Calvert himself, first mentioned by Rawnsley.

In 1994, a series of notebooks, the Fox How Magazines, belonging to the children of Dr Thomas Arnold of Rugby, written while they were staying on holiday at Fox How in Rydal, were bequeathed by Mary Moorman, G.M. Trevelyan's daughter, and herself a great-granddaughter of Thomas Arnold, Matthew's eldest brother. The Trust already owned letters to Wordsworth by Thomas Arnold, the Headmaster of Rugby, and they had acquired part of the manuscript of Matthew Arnold's 'Sohrab and Rustum'; this new material is charmingly and comically rhymed and illustrated by members of the family. The collection also contains many of the surviving photographs of the Arnold family.

Some surprising local collections have recently come to the Trust. The Green family of Pavement End, through J.M. Rees-Davies and his sister, Miss R.A. Rees-Davies, have given portraits, photographs and papers: their paintings of Mr and Mrs John Green are now in How Foot Lodge, a house built by the Greens, in 1843, as a speculative venture. The Benson Papers, which deal with the Benson estates in Grasmere and at Dove Nest, to the south of Ambleside, give insight into the local background in which Wordsworth lived. It is also a collection which illuminates the history of the twenty-two buildings in the hamlet of Town End, including Dove Cottage itself, which were once in the hands of the Benson family. One separate letter, of 1826, from Thomas De Quincey to Mrs Benson, has come to light, in which he expresses surprise that she thought of ending his tenancy at Dove Cottage: his surprise was the greater, he insisted, since it was his intention to put the property into good order at his own expense. He seems to have persuaded Mrs Benson to continue his lease for perhaps another ten years. An unexpected addition has been the gift, from David and Rothy O'Brien, of the diaries of Miss Winifred Borwick, who lived at No. 1 Lake Terrace – a splendid boarding-house – which now houses seven members of staff. Among other important gifts are watercolours donated by Helen Read in 1979. Earlier, in

1949, Beatrix Thornley had presented the wonderful Chubbard sketchbook of drawings of Rydal and Grasmere, dated from 1795–97. Even as we go to press, Symon and Shiela Brown (already benefactors of the Trust with generous loans of two of the finest William Blacklock paintings) have presented, in memory of their friend Timothy John Sewell, a mythic and moonlit watercolour of Thirlmere by W.G. Collingwood, c.1900, illustrating the lines in *The Waggoner* that describe the death of King Dunmail and the defeat of all his power in Viking times.

Even if the Trust's responsibilities in collecting material are not widely understood, it is clear is that the Trust has benefited greatly from generous donors. In 1994 the Wordsworth-Higginbotham family provided a series of family letters as well as portraits by William Boxall, Arthur Severn, and the painting by Beaumont of Coleorton which had inspired Wordsworth's sonnet: 'Praise be the art'. From another branch of the family, one hundred and fifty letters were secured with the help of Brian Enright, Librarian of the University of Newcastle upon Tyne, then a Trustee. Some of Richard Wordsworth's collection, entailed to him, was secured in 2003 with the help of the Friends of the National Libraries: a bound copy of the *1815 Poems* with additional text on unopened pages (bound up proof-sheets) was especially exciting. At the same time, over one million pounds has had to be raised in the last twenty years to acquire significant national treasures. Another instance was the manuscript of Wordsworth's *Ecclesiastical Sketches*, 1822, which had escaped from the Wordsworth family in the nineteenth century covered. The generosity of the Heritage Lottery Fund, together with the support of the W.W. Spooner Charitable Trust, made this acquisition possible. Equally interesting was a separate group of letters from the Wordsworth family to John Kenyon, best known as Dickens' friend, involving a discussion of Wordsworth's poetry and, perhaps explaining why Kenyon had borrowed the Wordsworth manuscripts in the fist place.

An unexpected group of material from various sources has been purchased relating to Thomas Wilkinson, the Quaker friend of the Clarksons, who became Wordsworth's colleague and friend, and who was engaged in supervising the landscaping of pathways round the River Emont in Lord Lonsdale's grounds. Wilkinson's portrait by Matthew Ellis Nutter gave us a work by a significant Cumberland artist; and, with it, came a painting of Wilkinson's house by his follower, Jacob Thompson (1806–1879), probably his first significant oil painting. That Wilkinson was the inspiration behind 'The Solitary Reaper' would have been enough to make him interesting to the

Trust. However, among the manuscripts that have appeared on the market is a description of an ascent of the Langdale Pikes in 1801, an important early mountaineering journal. His companion on this ascent was Elizabeth Smith of Coniston, a noted local author. Within Wilkinson's circle was the artist, Mary Dixon, described by the Hardens as 'the best female artist they knew'. Mary Dixon presented Thomas Wilkinson with a picture of her house and of Yanwath Hall, beside which Wilkinson's own house stood; they in turn were given to the Trust by Wilkinson's niece, Mary Carr.

As already noted, the Trust's fine art collection began with 'Grasmere' by White Abbott. In 1982 Cecil and Ann Parkinson helped the Trust acquire one of its greatest treasures – Francis Towne's watercolour, *Elterwater*, 1786. Two Constables were soon acquired (*Langdale Pikes* and *Helvellyn*), illuminating the importance of Constable's Lake District tour in 1806: they are major works in themselves. The acquisition drew attention to the important passage in Farington's Diary, 12 December 1807, in which he records that Wordsworth told Constable that he had had to hold onto a wall to make sure that he was in this world, so vigorous was his imaginative activity when a boy. The acquisition in 1984 of a group of Beaumont material relating to the Lake District – some 180 drawings – was complementary to the Constable material: Constable had visited Beaumont before coming to the Lakes and had seen his sketches. Another artist who had seen Beaumont's sketches was Thomas Girtin, and amongst the drawings was Girtin's brilliant 'improvement' of Beaumont's sketch of Borrowdale. Perhaps one of the Trust's greatest challenges was the purchase of Beaumont's painting of Peel Castle, which had gone to the United States. At £30,000, it was perhaps the most expensive of Beaumont's paintings, but as it was the painting that inspired one of the greatest English poems, Wordsworth's 'Elegiac Stanzas' on the death of his brother John, its price pales into insignificance. The greatest painting that the Trust has acquired is Joseph Wright of Derby's *Ullswater*. This is not only the last painting that Wright did, but it allows us to illustrate Wordsworth's great passage about stealing a boat on Ullswater as it depicts the scene of the incident. Wright, of course, did not know Wordsworth, nor Wordsworth Wright – but the excitement for the visitor comes from seeing the two great works of art, each powerful in their own way, enriching each other.

Another oil, among several major gifts of paintings and watercolours from Charles Warren, is that by David Cox of 1842, showing the crossing of Morecambe Bay Sands, which so admirably illuminates the passage in *The Prelude* (1805), X, 515–37) where Wordsworth describes the magnificence of the bay and his suddenly learning, by a casual enquiry, that Robespierre was dead. For Wordsworth, Robespierre was the malefactor who had turned the ideals of the French Revolution into blood and despair.

There is one passage in *The Prelude* (1805), VII, 311–46, concerned with Mary of Buttermere, a figure for whom Wordsworth felt deep sympathy as both had been brought up on the banks of the Cocker, the river that joins the Derwent at Cockermouth. He felt that her fate, to have been deceived into a bigamous marriage to James Hatfield, was wretched indeed. Mary had been famous before this 'marriage', largely because of James Budworth's praise of her in his *Ramble among the Lakes*, 1792 and 1795, and she had become a tourist attraction which people made it their business to visit (and to comment on). Thus, a relatively rare drawing by James Gillray, a cartoonist, apparently dated 1800, showing Mary in the inn with a face that is still beautiful, is of great interest. Gillray's image projects across a room in a most remarkable way. It was an equal pleasure to find a group of twenty-four drawings by Thomas Jameson (who first appears in Dorothy Wordsworth's Grasmere Journal as 'Little Tommy'). Supported by the Harden family, Jameson went briefly to the Royal Academy and was much influenced by William Green and William Havell. Equally, it was both a surprise and pleasure to come across three portraits of Havell, and one of that *doyen* of Lake District artists in the first twenty years of the nineteenth century, William Green: these pencil portraits were the work of John Varley, who seems to have been using the optical telescope of his brother, Cornelius. The pictures have a kind of photographic vitality.

Photographic images (including a magnificent set *c.*1870 by James Mudd of Manchester) abound in the Trust's collection; and so do the number of sculptures that the Trust holds. The Wordsworth bust by Thrupp, 1851, based on Haydon's drawing of 1819, was the gift of the Benson-Harrison family. The bust of Norman Nicholson was the gift of its maker, Josefina de Vasconcellos. Another of Josefina's gifts include her brilliant sculpture of two boys wrestling in the traditional Cumberland style, and Delmar Banner's remarkable painting of 'Scafell, Looking towards Great Gable'. The acquisition of our largest painting, J.B. Pyne's *Windermere from Orrest Head* (1851), is significant in showing the new railway which reached Windermere in 1847. The railway did not go further, not least because of Wordsworth's protests. Many wonders in the Trust's collections are illustrated in the catalogue that follows, but they are just tokens of a great wealth which, it is hoped, will feed the imagination of scholars and the general public for years to come.

Perhaps a key image to mention is the acquisition of Benjamin Robert Haydon's drawing of Wordsworth in 1819: it hung upon Haydon's wall and was seen by William Hazlitt on his frequent visits to Haydon. William Hazlitt is a hero to all who study the Romantics carefully. It is in Hazlitt's essay, 'On My First Acquaintance with Poets', that he gives a description of Wordsworth as he was in 1798, when the *Lyrical Ballads* were being written. After years of sniping at Wordsworth for his failure to live up to his earlier liberal, even revolutionary, principles, Hazlitt finally decided, in *The Spirit of the Age*, that Wordsworth, of all the poets, was the one who embodied that 'Spirit' best of all. He concludes his pen-portrait, which is illustrated in the catalogue, with the famous words that "Haydon's head of him, introduced into the *Entrance of Christ into Jerusalem*, is the most like his drooping weight of thought and expression".

The year 2004 saw the drawing together of many threads, not least in the area of books. The collections of manuscripts and works of art had been growing apace; and undoubtedly they are the reason the Trust can boast it has supported the publication of one scholarly book a month for the past ten years. It is a matter of pride that the editon of the collected Coleridge, and all the works that came from Kathleen Coburn and her team, could draw upon our collections. The scholarly achievements assisted by the Trust include the collected De Quincey, edited by Grevel Lindop; Duncan Wu's revision of the collected Hazlitt; Dorothy Wordsworth's *Alfoxden and Grasmere Journals*, re-edited by Pamela Woof; the great revision, in eight volumes, of *The Letters of William and Dorothy Wordsworth*, the task of over a quarter of a century, masterminded and finally completed by Professor Alan G. Hill. But the outstanding innovation in editorial presentation was the Cornell Wordsworth, a facsimile edition of Wordsworth's poetical manuscripts in twenty-one volumes, with Stephen Parrish as general editor, and a galaxy of the finest editors in his team. Biographies and critical studies on all the Romantic authors have abounded, and have been supported.

Always, however, there was a sense that the pursuit of single published volumes of the life-time editions of the great poets had not been so successfully achieved as had the purchases of manuscripts and fine art. Even so, by taking our opportunities, through the generosity of friends, the number of books in the Trust's collection have more than doubled. Edith Batho gave her collection of James Hogg; Ian Jack gave some choice items of Thomas de Quincey; Robert Gittings bequeathed his Keats library. Much helped by the John Finch Memorial Fund, we strategically arranged to purchase key works and some of the working collections of Ernest de Selincourt and Mary Moorman. As early as 1985 the purchase from James Dearden of his collection, dedicated to the area of Furness in the old county of Lancashire, had brought brilliant rarities (to name but one, the suppressed attack on John Bolton of Storrs, dated 1809, thought to have been completely destroyed); Dr Tim Wilson bequeathed to the Trust his collection centring on Charles Lamb and Leigh Hunt; Charles Warren and Peter Butter strengthened our now enviable collection of facsimiles of the works of William Blake; and the family of Oliver Turnbull gave us the heart of his literary collection, studded with stars, such as the first editions of most of the Brontë and George Eliot novels; the late Sir Francis à Court, with his wife Alison, by generous forethought, saw that this year we received his fine Coleridge collection; and in April 2004, at the opening of the exhibition based on Hazlitt's *Spirit of the Age*, the Rt Hon Michael Foot announced the bequest of his Hazlitt library, part of which is already with the Trust. Sir Eric Anderson, rightly sensing there was a weakness in the Trust's holdings of Sir Walter Scott, generously let us know that it was his intention to bequeath his collection of first editions of Scott – a bookcase of rarities, many of them triple-deckers! And Professor Michael C. Jaye (and his family) has, among other kindnesses over the years, sought out books and pictures which he knew would supplement the Trust's holdings, a remarkable support over twenty-five years.

In 2004, the acquisition of Geoffrey Bindman's collection (begun by his father in the 1920s) was successfully negotiated and, at a stroke, the Trust could more confidently assert its ambition to be *the* Museum of the Romantic Book. The Bindman collection is strong in the radical thinkers and political activists of the 1790s; it has near perfect holdings of Godwin, Mary Wollstonecraft, Mary Shelley and Shelley himself, and John Keats. Thomas Love Peacock, John Hamilton Reynolds, Charles and Mary Lamb, and Charles Lloyd are also strongly represented. The collection also includes some delicious rarities of Wordsworth, Coleridge, Hazlitt and Southey. More, the collection has a series of copies in original boards, a bibliographical aspect of collecting perhaps too much neglected since William Knight gave his beautifully bound volumes. An annotated copy of Southey's *Annual Anthology* includes Coleridge's annotations to his poem 'Lewti'. As this was a poem that Coleridge had worked up from an original poem by the schoolboy Wordsworth, we have a wonderful opportunity to compare the two versions side by side. There are 1,400 titles and 2,000 volumes. It was a magical and imaginative act of the North West Committee of the Heritage Lottery Fund to allow this collection to expand so magnificently, complementing what has been accumulated over one hundred years.

A final word must be said about some three-dimensional 'treasures'. The Wordsworth Bureau, purchased from Giles Wordsworth in 1982, is now on exhibition at Wordsworth House, Cockermouth, It took four years of careful craftsmanship to restore this wonderful example of provincial furniture (made in Cockermouth in 1766, with the latinised initials of Wordsworth's father, 'I.W'). In memory of his brother Giles, Jonathan Wordsworth presented a dressing-table mirror given to the Wordsworths by Lady Beaumont. And, again with the help of the Heritage Lottery Fund and the sustaining help of the Lakes Poets Society, the Trustees obtained the Coleridge / Southey collection from Greta Hall. This includes several family portraits by Mathilda Betham, Edward Nash and Caroline Bowles-Southey. Caroline's drawings of Greta Hall, both inside and outside, are a unique record; and among other items is the famous carved Southey chest which includes a 'cabinet of curiosities', offering an intriguing challenge for cataloguers which will doubtless take years to fully identify. A harp made of needles by Edith Southey was given in 2001 by Helen Muir in memory of her mother: the harp directly inspired Wordsworth's mock-heroic and complementary poem, which will delight every visitor.

I must end by conveying the Trustees' thanks to all, but especially the public institutions, who have supported these purchases. These include the Pilgrim Trust, who first funded our conservation work in 1970, which began with the appointment of that mastermind Sandy Cockerell as our conservator and consultant; after Sandy's death in 1988, we were fortunate to appoint Chris Clarkson. Over twenty years ago, we benefited enormously from the British Library Fund, the 1 3 B Scheme, supervised by Doris Crews and advised by Hilton Kelliher. Their work joined with the purposes of the National Heritage Memorial Fund under, Lord Charteris and Brian Laing, to allow conservation work on the growing collection to become a major commitment. Valuable support came from the Government funds administered by the Victoria and Albert Museum (now on behalf of MLA); from the National Art Collections Fund; from the Friends of the National Libraries; and, not least, from the Beecroft Bequest. But, recently, the timely help of the W.W. Spooner Charitable Trust, under its inspired Chairman, Michael Broughton, has raised the building of a collection of works by artists to a comprehensive level. It is these good people, and many of them have not been named, who have made this a collection of major importance and worthy of the fine building which has been funded by the Jerwood Founda-tion, the Heritage Lottery Fund, the Northwest Development Agency and the EEC. The Jerwood Centre at the Wordsworth Trust will ensure that the work of the Trust continues to be a living memorial to the poet, his contem-poraries, and a welcome resource to those who study Romanticism across the globe. Electronic access has been made possible by two major grants from the Designation Challenge Fund, administered by the MLA on behalf of the Department of Culture, Media and Sport. This work has been sup-ported, and continues to be aided, by many exceptional young people from all over the world who have come to Grasmere to take part in our volunteer and training programmes. All of their work over the years has depended upon enterprising librarians and curators; and if I name them, it is scarcely sufficient thanks, but it is thanks indeed: Phoebe Johnson, Nesta Clutter-buck, Stephen Gill (later Trustee Librarian), Peter Laver, Terry McCormick and, not least, our present Curator, the inimitable Jeff Cowton.

WILLIAM WORDSWORTH

William Wordsworth (1770–1850)

The Christabel Notebook

1797–1800   Manuscript

This notebook, bound in red leather, is a compendium of Wordsworth's poems brought together after his visit to Germany in 1798–9. It contains some of the earliest drafts of his great autobiographical poem *The Prelude*, including the lines invoking the River Derwent, which ran below the terrace walk in the garden of his childhood home in Cockermouth:

> was it for this
> That one the fairest of all rivers loved
> To blend his murmurs with my nurse's song
> And from his alder shades and rocky falls
> And from his fords and shallows sent a voice
>   That flowed along my
> To intertwine my ˄ dreams. For this didst thou,
> Oh Derwent, travelling over the green plains
> Near my sweet birth-place, didst thou, beauteous stream,
> ~~Murmur perpetual music~~ night and day,*
> Which with its steady cadence tempering
> Our human waywardness, composed my thoughts
> To more than infant softness, giving me
> Among the fretful dwellings of mankind
> A knowledge, a dim earnest, of the calm
> Which Nature breathes among her woodland haunts
>
> *Soon revised to: 'Make ceaseless music through the night and day'*

The notebook also contains the earliest surviving manuscript of Samuel Taylor Coleridge's 'Christabel', hence its name. This is in the hand of Mary Hutchinson (who was to become Wordsworth's wife in 1802), and was probably copied when Mary and Coleridge overlapped as guests at Dove Cottage, late February to early April 1800.

Gordon Graham Wordsworth Bequest, 1935

was it for this

That one the fairest of all rivers, loved
To blend his murmurs with my nurse's song
And from his alder shades and rocky falls
And from his fords and shallows sent a voice
That flowed along my dreams. For this didst thou
O Derwent travelling over the green plains
Near my sweet birth place didst thou beauteous stream
Make ceaseless music night and day
Which with its steady cadence tempering
Our human waywardness composed my thoughts
To more than infant softness giving me
Among the fretful dwellings of mankind
A knowledge a dim earnest of the calm
Which nature breathes among her woodlands
Blessed Derwent fairest of all streams
Was it for this that I the four years' child
A naked boy among thy silent pools
Made one long bathing of a summer's day
Basked in the sun or plunged into thy streams
Alternate all a summer's day or coursed
Over the sandy fields and dashed the flowers
Of yellow grunsel or when the hill-tops
The woods and all the distant mountains
Were browned with a deep radiance stood alone
A naked savage in the thunder shower.

      And afterwards, 'twas in a later day
Though early when upon the mountain slope
The frost and breath of frosty wind had snapped
The last autumnal crocus twas my joy
To wander half the night among the cliffs

[2] *Joseph Wright of Derby* (1734–1797)

Ullswater

c.1794–5   Oil on canvas, 44.4 × 52 cm

The scene depicted here of the southern reaches of Ullswater is the same setting as that used by Wordsworth for his description in *The Prelude* of the stealing of the boat while staying at Patterdale as a schoolboy:

> A rocky steep uprose
> Above the cavern of the willow-tree,
> And now, as suited one who proudly rowed
> With his best skill, I fixed a steady view
> Upon the top of that same craggy ridge,
> The bound of the horizon—for behind
> Was nothing but the stars and the grey sky.
> She was an elfin pinnace; lustily
> I dipped my oars into the silent lake,
> And as I rose upon the stroke my boat
> Went heaving through the water like a swan—
> When from behind that craggy steep, till then
> The bound of the horizon, a huge cliff,
> As if with voluntary power instinct,
> Upreared its head.

Wright's marvellous study of evening light shows the ranged shadows silhouetted against the sky: on the left-hand side the lower slope of Place Fell is shown, thought by some commentators to be the very hill that 'upreared its head' to the youthful Wordsworth's terror. A skiff, such as Wordsworth 'stole', is detectable in the central foreground. This is believed to be one of the last pictures Joseph Wright painted.

Purchased 1991, with the support of the MGC/V&A Purchase Grant Fund, the National Art Collections Fund, Sir Harry and Lady Djanogly, the J. Paul Getty Jr General Charitable Trust, Mrs Henry Luce III and the Luce Foundation, Mr Brian McElney, the Binks Trust, and Mr and Mrs Eugene Thaw

[3] *Sir James Lowther, 1st Earl of Lonsdale (1736–1802)*

Portrait by Thomas Hudson (1701–1779)

1755–6   Oil on canvas, 127 × 101.6 cm

'Wicked Jimmy', the 'Bad Earl', the 'Tyrant of the North', 'Jimmy Grasp-all, Earl of Toadstool' – some of the nicknames given to Sir James Lowther, the 1st Earl of Lonsdale, portrayed here in 'Vandyke' masquerade costume. 'He was truly a madman', concluded the Reverend Alexander Carlyle, 'but too rich to be confined'. His wealth was matched by his meanness, as is well illustrated in his treatment of the Wordsworth family. John Wordsworth, father of the poet, was his land-steward and law-agent at Cockermouth, and when he died in 1783 Sir James owed him £5,000 in legal and political fees. Despite six years of litigation Sir James refused to pay the money to the Wordsworth children, leaving them in near poverty, and it was not until after his death in 1802 that the poet and his brothers and sister received their dues (with full interest) from Sir James's successor.

Gift of C. Roy Huddleston, 1991

[4] *William Wordsworth*

'The Vale of Esthwaite'

1787   Manuscript

This notebook was mainly used for 'The Vale of Esthwaite', the poem
Wordsworth wrote at Hawkshead during the spring and summer of 1787,
just before going to Cambridge. The manuscript, in the poet's own hand,
is illustrated here at lines which twelve years later were reworked as one of
the great 'spots of time' episodes in *The Prelude*, describing the death of his
father:

> No spot but claims the tender tear
> By joy or grief to memory dear
> One Evening—when the wintery blast
> Through the sharp Hawthorn whistling passed
> And the poor flocks, all pinchd with cold
> Sad, drooping, sought the mountain fold
> naked
> Long Long, upon yon steepy rock
> Alone I bore the bitter shock
> Long Long, my swimming eyes did roam
> For little Horse to bear me home
> To bear me what avails my tear?
> To sorrow oer a Father's bier.—

While the 'bitter shock' primarily refers to the 'wintery' weather, it perhaps anticipates his father's death.

Gordon Graham Wordsworth Bequest, 1935

...ot but claims the tender tear
...oy or grief to memory dear
...vening when the wintery blast
...ough the sharp Hawthorn whistling passed
...d the poor flocks all pinched with cold
...a drooping sought the mountain fold
...ng long upon yon steepy rock
...lone I bore the bitter shock
...ng long my swimming eyes did scan
...or little horse to bear me home
...o bear me what avails my tear
...o sorrow oer a Father's bier —
...low on — in vain thou hast not flow'd
...but eas'd me of an heavy load
...or much it gives my soul relief
...o pay the mighty debt of Grief
...with sighs repeated oer and oer
...mourn because I mourn'd no more
...oor ...
...or died my little heart foresee
...he lost a home in losing thee
...or did it know of thee bereft
...hat little more than Heavn was left
    ...thanks to the voice in whisper sweet
...that says we soon again shall meet
...or oft when fades the leaden day
...o joy consuming pain a prey
...a horn afar the midnight bell
...flings on mine ear its solemn knell
...a still voice whispers to my breast
...soon shalt be with them that rest
    ...Then, mays some kind an pious friend
...his tears oer my body bend.

[5] *William Wordsworth*

An Evening Walk

London: J. Johnson, 1793

An Evening Walk was Wordsworth's first book. A picturesque evocation of
the Lake District in heroic couplets, it was completed in the Cambridge
summer vacation of 1789, and printed by the radical publisher Joseph
Johnson with *Descriptive Sketches* [see no. 6]. This copy was inscribed by
Wordsworth, aged seventy-five, to his son William:

> Part of this Poem was composed at School and was published at the
> same time as the "Descriptive Sketches" a good deal of which latter
> Piece was composed in France during the year 1792. Previous to the
> appearance of these two Attempts I had not published any thing, except
> a Sonnet printed in the European Magazine June or July 1786 when I was
> [a] School-Boy. The Sonnet was signed Axiologus—Wm Wordsworth 16
> March 1846. Rydal Mount.

An Evening Walk is written in an eighteenth-century Augustan manner,
and borrows from poets such as Milton, Pope, Thomson and Gray, but it
is based on Wordsworth's own knowledge and experience of the Lakes.
'There is not an image in it which I have not observed', he later said, 'and
now, in my seventy-third year, I recollect the time and place where most of
them were noticed'.

Gordon Graham Wordsworth Bequest, 1935

A N

EVENING WALK.

An EPISTLE;

IN VERSE.

ADDRESSED TO A YOUNG LADY,

FROM THE

LAKES

OF THE

NORTH OF ENGLAND.

BY

W. WORDSWORTH, B. A.

Of St. JOHN's, CAMBRIDGE.

LONDON:

PRINTED FOR J. JOHNSON, St. PAUL's CHURCH-YARD.
1793.

William Wordsworth
Rydal
Mount   *his affectionate Father*
16 March   *Wm Wordsworth*
1846

[6] *William Wordsworth*

Descriptive Sketches

London: J. Johnson, 1793

Descriptive Sketches was published by Joseph Johnson in January 1793 as was *An Evening Walk*. The poem was written in France in 1792, partly under the influence of Michel Beaupuy, the French army officer who converted Wordsworth to the ideals of the Revolution. It takes the form of a picturesque tour based on the poet's walking tour of France and the Alps during the summer vacation of 1790, but ends as a declaration of faith in liberty and the Revolution:

> Lo! from th'innocuous flames, a lovely birth!
> With its own virtues, springs another earth:
> Nature, as in her prime, her virgin reign
> Begins, and Love and Truth compose her train.

Descriptive Sketches seems to have been the first of Wordsworth's poems to catch the attention of Coleridge, who saw in it a mixture of harshness and 'images all a-glow … The language was not only peculiar and strong, but at times knotty and contorted, as by its own impatient strength; while the novelty and struggling crowd of images acting in conjunction with the difficulties of the style, demanded always a greater closeness of attention, than poetry, (at all events, than descriptive poetry) has a right to claim' (*Biographia Literaria*, 1817).

This copy was formerly in the collection of Cynthia Morgan St. John, the founder of the Wordsworth collection now at Cornell University. The initials 'T.F.T.' have not been identified.

From the collection of Cynthia Morgan St. John

DESCRIPTIVE SKETCHES.

IN VERSE.

TAKEN DURING A

PEDESTRIAN TOUR

IN THE

ITALIAN, GRISON, SWISS, AND SAVOYARD

A L P S.

BY

W. WORDSWORTH, B. A.

Of St. JOHN's, CAMBRIDGE.

—Loca paſtorum deſerta atque otia dia.

LUCRET.

Caſtella in tumulis—
—Et longe ſaltus lateque vacantes.

VIRGIL.

L O N D O N:

PRINTED FOR J. JOHNSON, ST. PAUL's CHURCH-YARD.
1793.

[7] *William Wordsworth*

The Windy Brow Notebook

1792–4   Manuscript

This notebook is largely made up of work composed between 1792 and 1794, and transcribed by Wordsworth and Dorothy when they were staying together at Windy Brow farmhouse near Keswick in spring 1794. It includes extracts from 'An Evening Walk' and, primarily, 'A Night on Salisbury Plain'. The watermark is an image of Britannia in a crowned oval, and the counter-mark is the monogram 'JA' in a double circle containing the inscription 'Cowan Head'.

Wordsworth's three-day walk across Salisbury Plain took place in August 1793. The poem he began to compose as he walked is mainly an im-passioned protest against the war with France. Stone Age life on Salisbury Plain and the horrors of human sacrifice (associated with the Druids, and assumed to have taken place at Stonehenge) form the backdrop of a poem about war and the barbarism of contemporary society:

> Hard is the life when naked and unhoused
> And wasted by the long day's fruitless pains
> thickets
> The hungry savage 'mid deep forests roused
> By storms, lies down at night on unknown plains
> And lifts his head in fear while famished trains
> Of boars along the crashing forests prowl—
> And, heard in darkness as the rushing rains
> Put out his watch-fire, bears contending growl
> And round his fenceless bed gaunt wolves in armies howl.

Gordon Graham Wordsworth Bequest, 1935

A night

Salisbury Plain on Salisbury plain

Salisbury plain.

Hard is the life when naked

Hard is the life when naked and unhoused
And wasted by the long day's fruitless pains
The hungry savage 'mid deep forests, roused.
By storms, lies down at night on unknown
And lifts his head in fear while famished trains plains
Of boars along the crashing forests prowl thickets
And heard in darkness as the rushing rains
Put out his watch-fire bears contending growl
And round his fenceless bed gaunt wolves

in armies howl

2

was that some poison cup

is he strong to suffer & his mind
Encounters all his evils unsubdued
happier days since at the breast he his
never knew, and when by foes pursued

[8] *David Cox (1783–1859)*

Morecambe Bay, Lancaster Sands

1842 Oil on canvas, 33 × 48 cm

David Cox was primarily a watercolourist and drawing master, who achieved popularity through a series of influential drawing books. He first visited Lancaster Sands in 1834, and from 1835 to 1847 produced a number of both watercolours and oils on the subject of travellers making the dangerous crossing from Lancashire to what is now Cumbria. It was while crossing the sands in 1794 that Wordsworth heard of Robespierre's death; he recalled in Book X of *The Prelude* (1805):

> … all the plain
> Was spotted with a variegated crowd
> Of coaches, wains, and travellers, horse and foot,
> Wading, beneath the conduct of their guide,
> In loose procession through the shallow stream
> Of inland water; the great sea meanwhile
> Was at safe distance, far retired. I paused,
> Unwilling to proceed, the scene appeared
> So gay and chearful—when a traveller
> Chancing to pass, I carelessly inquired
> If any news were stirring, he replied
> In the familiar language of the day
> That, *Robespierre was dead*. Nor was a doubt,
> On further question, left within my mind
> But that the tidings were substantial truth—
> That he and his supporters all were fallen.
> Great was my glee of spirit, great my joy
> In vengeance, and eternal jusice, thus
> Made manifest. 'Come now ye golden times,'
> Said I, forth-breathing on those open Sands
> A hymn of triumph …

Gift of Charles Warren, 1990

[9] *William Wordsworth*

'The Ruined Cottage'

1798   Manuscript

This home-made notebook contains Dorothy Wordsworth's transcription
of the first complete text of 'The Ruined Cottage', the last of Wordsworth's
Racedown poems and the greatest of his narratives of human suffering. In
simple terms, it tells how the poet meets by chance a recent acquaintance,
a pedlar, at the ruined cottage. The Pedlar, a figure of considerable dignity,
tells, with some of the particularity we expect from a novelist, the tale of
the abandoned Margaret's suffering, Margaret being 'the last human tenant
of these ruined walls'. Wordsworth establishes by the end of the poem
that the poet, having heard the story, is no longer indifferent to the ruined
cottage – its neglected garden, its weeds of spear-grass, its well. In all these
objects the poet discovers

> That secret spirit of humanity
> Which, 'mid the calm oblivious tendencies
> Of nature, 'mid her plants, her weeds, and flowers,
> And overgrowings, still survived.

The dead woman, the poet and the place are in a relationship which has
been born out of the story-teller's art. Increasingly, Wordsworth, the
subtle psychiatrist, finds strategies to expose man's inhumanity to man; but
equally, he also wants to display the good relationship between the Poet
and the Pedlar (who tells the tale) and the wise Pedlar's relationship with
the living universe. As ever, Wordsworth's concern is with the life of the
mind.

Gordon Graham Wordsworth Bequest, 1935

The   wall where that same gaudy
                                              Flower
Lashed out upon the road. It was a plot
Of garden-ground now wild {to matted weed
                          just as when
Marked with the steps of those who as
                                   they pass
The gooseberry trees that shot in long
                  hanging from their
Or currents ~~hung~~ on leafless stems
      For
~~their~~ scanty strings had tempted to
                                   o'er leap
The broken wall. Within that cheerless ~~pl~~

Where two tall hedgerows of thick willow boughs

Joined in a damp cold nook I found a well

Half choaked

I slaked my thirst & to the shady bench
Returned & while I stood unbonneted
To catch the current of the breezy air
The old man said "I see around me
Things which you cannot see. We die my
                                  each   friend
Nor we alone but that which man loved

131

William Wordsworth

The Alfoxden Notebook

1797–1802   Manuscript

This manuscript notebook was used by Wordsworth at Alfoxden between January and March 1798. It is open here at the first draft of 'The Thorn' – one of the few manuscripts in Wordsworth's hand that survives of poems published in *Lyrical Ballads*, 1798:

> A summit where the stormy gale
> Sweeps through the clouds from vale to vale
> A thorn there is which like a stone
> With jagged lychens overgrown
> A thorn that wants its thorny points
> A toothless thorn with knotted joints
> 'Tis old & grey and low and wild
> Not higher that a two years' child
> It stands upon that spot so wild
> Of leaves it has repaired its loss
> With heavy tufts of dark green moss
> Which from the ground in plenteous crop
> Creeps upward to its very top

The lines on the lower half of the page were used to form a second poem, 'A whirl-blast from behind the hill', published in the 1800 edition of *Lyrical Ballads*. On 19th March 1798 Dorothy recorded in her Journal that 'William wrote some lines describing a stunted thorn', and on the day before she noted his writing 'a description of the storm'.

Gordon Graham Wordsworth Bequest, 1935

A summit where the stormy gale
Sweeps through the clouds from vale
                                    to vale
A thorn there is which like a stone
With jagged lychens overgrown
A thorny that wants is thorny froom
A troubled those with knotted
                                    joints
xxxx & grey, and lowand wilde
Not higher than is two years child
It stands, upon that spot so wild
of leaves it has repaired its loss
With heavy tufts of dark green moss
Which from the ground a plentioung
Creeps upward to it very top
                                    looks

I bury it for ever more

The wind sent from behind the hill
passes over the wood with rushing wing
xxx all at once the air was still
And showers of hailstones pattered round
Where xxxx xxx towered high
                                    alone
I rate within an undergrown
of tallest hollies tall & green
A fairer bower was never seen

[11] *Francis Nicholson (1753–1844)*

Tintern Abbey

1804 Watercolour, 44.5 × 32.3 cm

A preliminary sketch for this watercolour, also in the Trust's collection, is dated 14 July 1798. Nicholson therefore seems to have been at Tintern Abbey on or about the same day as Wordsworth and Dorothy. Wordsworth's great poem 'Lines written a few miles above Tintern Abbey while revisiting the Banks of the Wye' is dated 13 July, but he later declared that it took him three days to write the poem and he was uncertain whether 13 July was the day on which he started the poem or finished it.

This is one of two highly finished watercolours that Nicholson made of the abbey, probably for exhibition. It wonderfully presents the single unifying hue of green, so typical of the month of July, that characterises Wordsworth's description in the opening of 'Tintern Abbey'. One notes that the Abbey itself is present only in the title, as, at once, a map reference and a subtle indicator that the landscape 'a few miles above Tintern Abbey' has also a religious significance.

'The enchanting beauties of the River Wye are by this time pretty generally known among the lovers of the picturesque' wrote John Thelwall in the *New Monthly Magazine*, May 1798. 'They have acquired a due celebrity from the descriptions of GILPIN, and curiosity has been inflamed by poetry and by prose, by paintings, prints and drawings, till they have been rendered a subject of universal conversation. Such is the popularity of the Wye that an excursion on the river has become an essential part of the education, as it were, of all who aspire to the reputation of elegance, taste and fashion'. The Bertram girls clearly had such aspirations, for Jane Austen's Fanny Price cherished in her cold attic room at Mansfield Park 'three transparencies, made in a rage for transparencies'. These were placed in 'the three lower panes of one window, where Tintern Abbey held its station between a cave in Italy, and a moonlight lake in Cumberland.'

Purchased 1986, with the support of the MGC/V&A Purchase Grant Fund

[12] *William Wordsworth and Samuel Taylor Coleridge*

Lyrical Ballads

London: J. and A. Arch, 1798

In November 1797 Wordsworth and Coleridge, while walking with Dorothy in the Quantock Hills, conceived a plan to raise money. Within twelve months, they had composed a series of poems which were published by their friend Joseph Cottle as the *Lyrical Ballads* (Bristol 1798). In this volume the creative visions of each poet were complementary; Coleridge sought to give the supernatural an every day reality as in 'The Ancient Mariner', and Wordsworth's aim was to give ordinary experience a power equal to that of the supernatural. The *Lyrical Ballads* were to broaden our human sympathies and to show that delicacy and depth of feeling was not limited to any one class of men or women.

Overstretched financially, Cottle sold *Lyrical Ballads* to the London booksellers J. and A. Arch before publication. A new title page had to be printed and inserted, as here, as a cancel, and copies with the original Bristol imprint are extremely rare. This London copy has the following inscription by Wordsworth: 'This volume was published in conjunction with Mr Coleridge, at Bristol, by our common friend Mr Cottle, and immediately before its publication Mr Coleridge my sister and I went into Germany. The above memorandum is written to gratify my dear nephew John Wordsworth. Rydal Mount March 6 1844 Wm Wordsworth'.

Gift of Dorothy Dickson, 1967

LYRICAL BALLADS,

WITH

A FEW OTHER POEMS.

LONDON:

PRINTED FOR J. & A. ARCH, GRACECHURCH-STREET,

1798.

[13] *William and Dorothy Wordsworth*

Letter to Samuel Taylor Coleridge

14–21 December 1798   Manuscript

This letter to Coleridge was written while the Wordsworths were in Goslar, Germany. Isolated, and confined indoors by the severest winter for over a century, Wordsworth turned his thoughts to writing, and to his childhood in the Lake District: 'As I have had no books I have been obliged to write in self-defence' he tells Coleridge. 'I should have written five times as much as I have done, but that I am prevented by an uneasiness at my stomach and side, with a dull pain about my heart. I have used the word pain, but uneasiness and heat are words which more accurately express my feeling. At all events it renders writing unpleasant. Reading is now become a kind of luxury to me. When I do not read I am absolutely consumed by thinking and feeling and bodily exertions of voice or of limbs, the consequence of those feelings.'

On to the other side of the sheet (illustrated here) Dorothy has crammed what Wordsworth offhandedly describes as 'two or three little Rhyme poems which I hope will amuse you', and, in Dorothy's phrase, 'a few descriptions of William's boyhood pleasures'. These are, respectively, two of the 'Lucy' poems ('She dwelt among the untrodden ways' and 'Strange fits of passion'), 'Nutting' and two of the most important episodes from *The Prelude*: skating on Esthwaite, and the moonlit adventure on Ullswater.

Gordon Graham Wordsworth Bequest, 1935

Of hazles, and the green & mossy bower,
Deform'd & sullied, patiently gave up
their quiet spirit, & while I see
compared my present being with the past,
even then, when from the bower I turned away,
Regretting, rich bestow'd the wealth of things,
I felt a sense of pain when I beheld
The silent trees & the intruding sky —
Then, dearest Maiden! move along these shades
In gentleness of heart, with gentle hand
Touch, for there is a spirit in the woods

[14]   *Amos Green (1735–1807)*

Town End

*c.*1806   Watercolour, 13.1 × 20.3 cm

This the earliest picture of Dove Cottage and the hamlet of Town End. Wordsworth and Dorothy arrived here on the evening of 20 December 1799. 'D is much pleased with the house and *appurtenances* the orchard especially' Wordsworth wrote to Coleridge on Christmas Eve, 'in imagination she has already built a seat with a summer shed on the highest platform in this our little domestic slip of mountain. The spot commands a view over the roof of our house, of the lake, the church, helm cragg, and two thirds of the vale. We mean also to enclose the two or three yards of ground between us and the road, this for the sake of a few flowers, and because it will make it more our own.'

The Wordsworths lived at the Town End cottage (much later called Dove Cottage) until 1808. John, their sailor brother, was there until September 1800, Mary and Sara Hutchinson and Coleridge were frequent visitors, Mary marrying Wordsworth in October 1802. Three of the Wordsworths' five children were born here: John, Dora and Thomas. Other visitors included Walter Scott, Sir George Beaumont, Thomas De Quincey (who succeeded Wordsworth as tenant). After July 1800 Coleridge became almost a neighbour, living with his family at Greta Hall, Keswick.

The years at Dove Cottage were Wordsworth's most productive as a poet. Among the poems written at Dove Cottage are 'Michael', 'The Brothers', 'Ode: Intimations of Immortality', 'Resolution and Independence' and the thirteen-book *Prelude*, completed in 1805.

A copy of this picture was made by Dora Wordsworth in about 1826.

Gordon Graham Wordsworth Bequest, 1935

[15] *William Wordsworth*

'Home at Grasmere'

1806   Manuscript

Wordsworth began this poem in 1800 to celebrate his and Dorothy's with-drawal to Grasmere. He remembers his first sight of Grasmere as a school-boy rambling over the hills from Hawkshead. Looking down at the lake and valley from Red Bank on Loughrigg, he saw it as paradise:

> Once on the brow of yonder Hill I stopped
> While I was yet a School-boy (of what age
> I cannot well remember, but the hour
> I well remember though the year be gone),
> And, with a sudden influx overcome
> At sight of this seclusion, I forgot
> My haste, for hasty had my footsteps been
> As boyish my pursuits; and sighing said,
> 'What happy fortune were it here to live!
> And if I thought of dying, if a thought
> Of mortal separation could come in
> With paradise before me, here to die.'

Grasmere was perfect, a 'Centre', a 'Whole without dependence or defect', a 'blended holiness of earth and sky', an 'abiding place' of 'Perfect Content-ment, Unity entire'. These were high claims, and could hardly be sustained, even within the poem, which remained unfinished. It is a personal and, interestingly, a somewhat confused statement about Wordsworth's own position on returning, a man of outside education and experience, to the place at once paradisal, and, as he now noticed, subtly fallen.

Though almost the whole of the poem was written in 1800, this manu-script of 1806, entitled 'Recluse Book first', is the first complete fair copy. The handwriting is Mary Wordsworth's, with corrections by Wordsworth.

Gordon Graham Wordsworth Bequest, 1935

~~Isolated~~
Recluse

Book first

to the brow of yonder ~~steep, while~~
Once on ~~the brow of yonder~~ hill I stopp'd
I came - a roving
~~Holy I was yet~~ a School-boy (of what age
~~Math now escaped my memory~~
~~I cannot well remember~~ but the hour
I well remember though the year be gone
And with a sudden influx overcome
At sight of this seclusion I forgot
My haste for hasty had my footsteps been
As boyish my pursuits; and ~~ere~~
~~as yet the~~
What happy fortune were it here to live
And if I thought of dying if a thought
Of mortal separation could come ~~in~~
With paradise before me here to die.
I was no Prophet nor had even a hope
Scarcely a wish, but one bright pleasing thought
A fancy in the heart of what might be
The lot of others never could be mine.

16

William Wordsworth

Lines from 'Michael'

1800   Manuscript

Wordsworth was using this interleaved copy of Coleridge's *Poems* (1796) as a rough notebook in 1800. It contains work on 'Home at Grasmere' and drafts of 'Michael'. This poem tells of the lives of an old shepherd, his wife Isobel and only son Luke on their Grasmere farm. In order to retain his land Michael is forced to send Luke to London to earn money. The first stone of an unbuilt sheepfold placed by Luke and to be continued by his father is Michael's pledge for his son's return. Luke falls into dissolute ways and never returns; the sheepfold remains unfinished. Wordsworth described his intentions in writing 'Michael' and another poem, 'The Brothers', in a letter to the Whig politician Charles James Fox:

> I have attempted to draw a picture of the domestic affections as I know they exist amongst a class of men who are now almost confined to the North of England. They are small independent *proprietors* of land here called statesmen, men of respectable education who daily labour on their own little properties. The domestic affections will always be strong amongst men who live in a country not crowded with population, if these men are placed above poverty. But if they are proprietors of small estates, which have descended to them from their ancestors, the power which these affections will acquire amongst such men is inconceivable by those who have only had an opportunity of observing hired labourers, farmers, and the manufacturing Poor. Their little tract of land serves as a kind of permanent rallying point for their domestic feelings, as a tablet upon which they are written which makes them objects of memory in a thousand instances when they would otherwise be forgotten. ... The two poems which I have mentioned were written with a view to shew that men who do not wear fine cloaths can feel deeply.

Gordon Graham Wordsworth Bequest, 1935

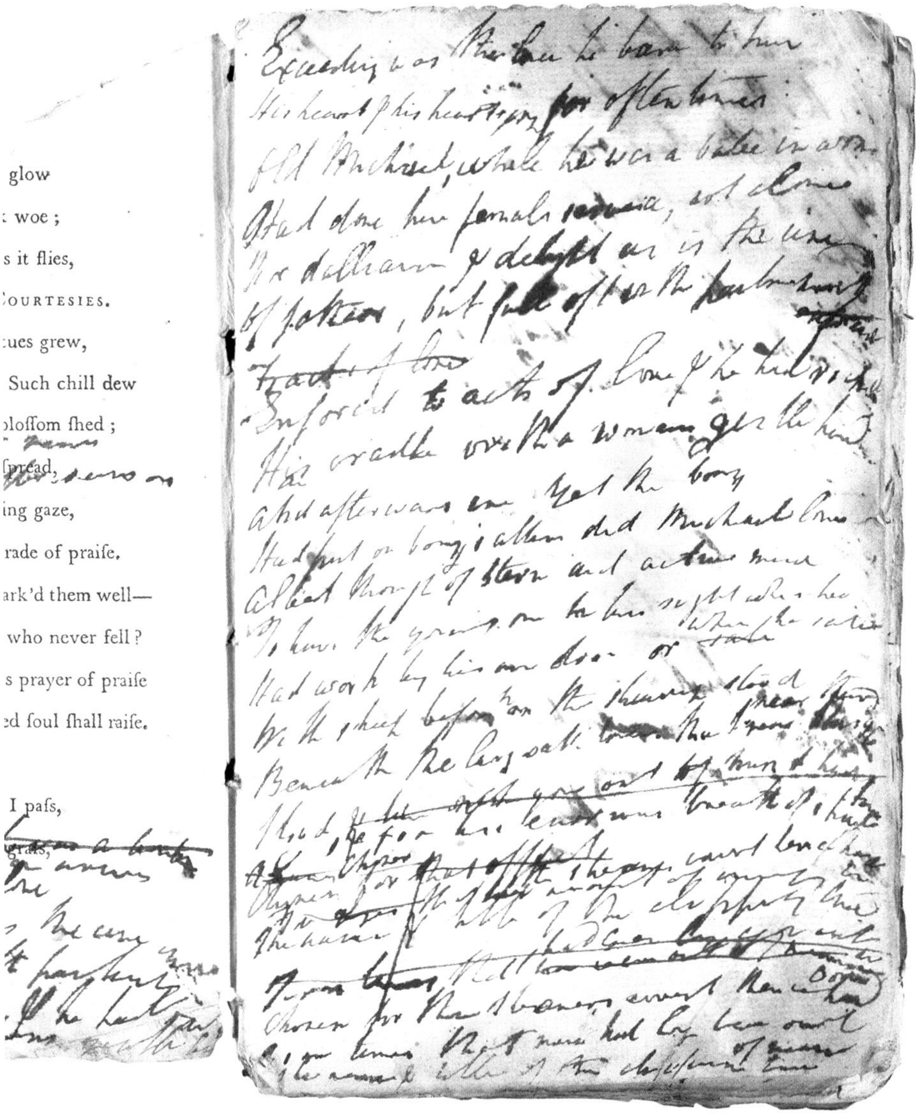

glow

woe ;

s it flies,

OURTESIES.

ues grew,

Such chill dew

lossom shed ;

spread,

ing gaze,

rade of praise.

ark'd them well—

who never fell ?

s prayer of praise

ed soul shall raise.

I pass,

17

William Wordsworth

Lyrical Ballads, with other poems

London: T. N. Longman and O. Rees, 1800

There are two black tulips amongst Wordsworth books. First is *Lyrical Ballads*, 1798, with the Bristol title-page, of which only some dozen copies are known. Rarer still is the second edition of *Lyrical Ballads*, 1800, where Wordsworth states on page 2 that Coleridge has written 'Christabel' for the volume.

Famously, by October 1800, Coleridge found himself unable to finish 'Christabel' – perhaps because his own unhappy marriage made it impossible for him to imagine the happy ending that the romance form of the story demanded. Christabel's lover ought to return and rescue her. As it is, the poem survives as a marvellous fragment in that it presents, in its very incompleteness, a wasteland image. The incomplete and therefore unpublished 'Christabel' of 1800 clearly prefigures Coleridge's next great poem, the Verse Letter to Sara Hutchinson of April 1802, which is subsequently edited down to the ode appropriately entitled 'Dejection'.

This rare copy of *Lyrical Ballads*, 1800, contains the original first leaf of the volume containing the announcement of 'Christabel', as well as the leaf (called a 'cancel') which was to replace it. Technically, the first leaf should be termed a 'slip'; there is a tear halfway up the page from the bottom and this was to show the binder that he must replace this page. Carelessly, the binder has not removed the page and in addition has bound the cancel in the wrong place. Wordsworth was anxious to have the book published in 1800, but despite all efforts it was not out until January 1801.

Wordsworth himself had had to set to in October to compose a long poem to replace 'Christabel'. This poem was 'Michael', not finished until 9 December 1800, and then so hurriedly and badly printed that further errors and cancels appeared in the second volume of *Lyrical Ballads*, 1800.

Purchased 1996, with the support of the National Heritage Memorial Fund, the Friends of the National Libraries, and Francis and Alison À Court

on the other hand I was well aware that by those who should dislike them they would be read with more than common dislike. The result has differed from my expectation in this only, that I have pleased a greater number, than I ventured to hope I should please.

For the sake of variety and from a consciousness of my own weakness I have again requested the assistance of a Friend who contributed largely to the first volume,* and who has now furnished me with the Poem of Christabel, without which I should not yet have ventured to present a second volume to the public. I should not however have requested this assistance, had I not believed that the poems of my Friend would in a great measure have the same tendency as my own, and that,

---

* The Poems supplied by my Friend, are the ANTIENT MARINER, the FOSTER-MOTHER'S TALE, the NIGHTIN-GALE, the DUNGEON, and the Poem entitled, LOVE.

[18]   *Dorothy Wordsworth (1771–1855)*

Portrait by an unknown artist

c.1806   Silhouette, 7.6 × 5.8 cm

This silhouette is inscribed in pencil on the reverse in the hand of Elizabeth Cookson: 'Miss Wordsworth / Sister of W.W.'. It is the only surviving portrait of Dorothy as a young woman, but conveys little of the animation and sensitivity that so struck people. Thomas De Quincey described her as having a 'Gipsy Tan', and eyes which were 'not soft like Mrs W's, nor bold: but they were wild and startling, and hurried in their motion. Her manner was warm and even ardent; her sensibility seemed constitutionally deep; and some subtle fire of impassioned intellect apparently burned within her …'. 'Wordsworth and his exquisite sister are with me', wrote Coleridge from Nether Stowey in June 1797,

> She is a woman indeed: in mind I mean, and heart; for her person is such that if you expected to see a pretty woman, you would think her ordinary; if you expected to see an ordinary woman you would think her pretty! But her manners are simple, ardent, impressive. In every motion her most innocent soul beams out so brightly, that who saw would say 'Guilt was a thing impossible in her'. Her information various. Her eye watchful in minutest observation of nature; and her taste a perfect electrometer. It bends, protrudes, and draws in, at subtlest beauties and most recondite faults.

In 1818 John Keats called at Rydal Mount while on his walking tour of the Lake District and Scotland. Finding no one at home, he left a note on the mantlepiece, propped against a portrait which he took to be of Wordsworth's sister. This portrait, assuming that it was, as Keats supposed, of Dorothy, has not survived.

Purchased 1970 from the Quin family (descended from the Cooksons of Kendal)

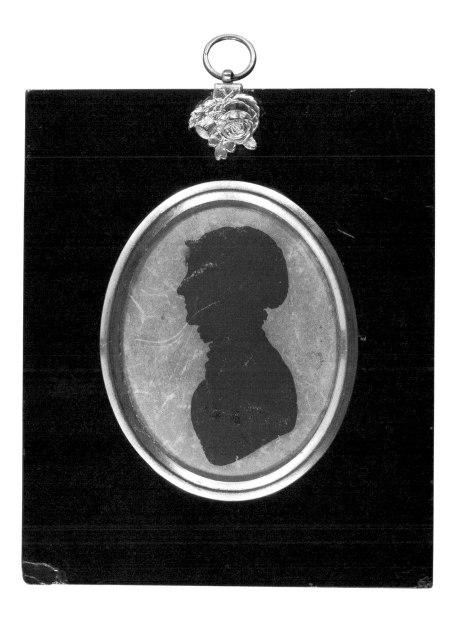

[19] *Dorothy Wordsworth (1771–1855)*

Journal

14 February – 2 May 1802   Manuscript

Dorothy Wordsworth's famous Grasmere Journals are contained in four notebooks, all held by the Wordsworth Trust. They cover the periods from 14 May to 22 December 1800 and from 10 October 1801 to 16 January 1803. Shown here is part of the entry for 15 April 1802 describing the wild daffodils by Ullswater, later a source for perhaps Wordsworth's best-known poem, 'I wandered lonely as a cloud':

> When we were in the woods beyond Gowbarrow park we saw a few daffodils close to the water side, we fancied that the lake had floated the seeds ashore & that the little colony had so sprung up—But as we went along there were more & yet more & at last under the boughs of the trees, we saw that there was a long belt of them along the shore, about the breadth of a country turnpike road. I never saw daffodils so beautiful they grew among the mossy stones about & about them, some rested their heads upon these stones as on a pillow for weariness & the rest tossed & reeled & danced & seemed as if they verily laughed with the wind that blew upon them over the Lake, they looked so gay ever glancing ever changing. This wind blew directly over the Lake to them. There was here & there a little knot & a few stragglers a few yards higher up but they were so few as not to disturb the simplicity & unity & life of that one busy highway—We rested again & again. The Bays were stormy & we heard the waves at different distances & in the middle of the water like the Sea—Rain came on ...

Dorothy's writing is considered and careful – witness her crossings out and insertions – but she brings an immediacy and a human life to the wind-blown daffodils. Her direct approach to the experience differs significantly from her brother's more distant recollection and re-creation of the scene.

Gordon Graham Wordsworth Bequest, 1935

& at last under the boughs
of the trees we saw that there
was a long belt of them ~
~~somewhere~~ along the
shore, about the breadth
of a country turnpike road.
I never saw daffodils so
beautiful they grew among
the mossy stones about & above
them, some rested their heads
upon these stones as on a
pillow for weariness & the
rest tossed & reeled & danced
& seemed as if ~~they verily~~
laughed with the wind ~~that~~
blew ~~upon~~ them ~~over the lake~~ they looked so gay ever glancing
~~ever changing~~ there was
here & there a little knot
and a few stragglers a few
yards higher up but they
were so few as not to disturb

[20] *Dorothy Wordsworth (1771–1855)*

Journal

May 1802 – January 1803   Manuscript

Dorothy Wordsworth's retrospective account in her Journal of her feelings
on the morning of Wordsworth's wedding-day, 4 October 1802. A number
of lines have been heavily crossed out in an attempt to make them impossible to read. A reading under infra-red light was obtained in the 1950s; a
possible alternative reading of the last four words within the square brack-
ets has recently been suggested: 'as I blessed the ring softly' (see Dorothy
Wordsworth, *The Grasmere and Alfoxden Journals*, ed. Pamela Woof, Oxford
World's Classics, 2002, p. xxvii and pp.265–6).

> I slept a good deal of the night & rose fresh & well in the morning—at a
> little after 8 o clock I saw them go down the avenue towards the Church.
> William had parted from me up stairs. [*crossed out* I gave him the wed-
> ding ring—with how deep a blessing! I took it from my forefinger where
> I had worn it the whole of the night before—he slipped it again onto
> my finger and blessed me fervently.] When they were absent my dear
> little Sara prepared the breakfast. I kept myself as quiet as I could, but
> when I saw the two men running up the walk, coming to tell us it was
> over, I could stand it no longer & threw myself on the bed where I lay &
> I moved I knew not how straight forward, faster than my strength could
> carry me till I met my beloved William & fell upon his bosom.

Dorothy welcomed the marriage of her brother to her best friend Mary
Hutchinson. She had been with Wordsworth in Calais in August when the
ring was bought and agreements reached with Annette Vallon, mother of
Wordsworth's daughter Caroline. She blessed the ring once, perhaps twice,
but of course she had known that the marriage would make a change:
'happy as I am, I half dread that concentration of all tender feelings, past,
present and future which will come upon me on the wedding morning.'

Gordon Graham Wordsworth Bequest, 1935

and were quiet & still in the morning at a little after 9 o'clock I saw them go down the Avenue towards the Church. William had parted from me up stairs, ~~crossed out~~ ~~crossed out~~ ~~crossed out~~ ~~crossed out~~ ~~crossed out~~ ~~crossed out~~. When "they were absent my dear" little Sara prepared the breakfast. I kept myself as quiet as I could, but when I saw the ~~dew~~ them running up the walk, ~~coming~~ to tell us it was over, I could stand it no longer & threw myself on the bed where I lay in stillness, neither hearing or seeing anything, till Sara came up stairs to me & said "they are coming –" This ~~forced~~ me from the bed where I lay & I moved I knew not how straight forward.

[21] *William Wordsworth*

Letter to Mary Wordsworth

22 July 1810   Manuscript

We do not think of Wordsworth primarily as a love poet. Because he and his wife had known each other for so long before they married, it has been assumed that their relationship was not especially close. A correspondence between them that came to light in 1978 shows a very different picture. It seems that in his brief absences from home Wordsworth had tended to send letters jointly to Mary and Dorothy, or to the family as a whole. On a visit to his brother-in-law, Tom Hutchinson, in summer 1810 he wrote directly to Mary. Her answer speaks for itself:

> Dorothy has asked me more than once when she has found me this morning with thy letter in my hand 'what I was crying about?' I told her that I was so happy, but she could not comprehend this. Indeed, my love, it has made me supremely blessed—it has given me a new feeling, for it is the first letter of love that has been exclusively my own. ... And I am sorry for what causes in me such pious and exalting gladness—that you cannot fully enjoy your absence from me. Indeed William I feel I have felt that you cannot, but it overpowers me to be told it by your own pen. I was much moved by the lines written with your hand in one of D's letters, where you spoke of coming home thinking you 'would be of great use' to me. Indeed, my love, thou woudst, but I did not want thee so much then, as I do now that our uncomfortableness has passed away—that underconsciousness that I had my all in all about me—that feeling which I have never wanted since the solitary night did not sepa-rate us, except in absence (but I had not then that leisure which I ought to have, and which is necessary to be actively alive to so rich a posses-sion, and to the full enjoyment of it. I do, William, and I shall to the end of my life, consider this sacrifice as a dear offering of thy love. I feel it to be such, and I am grateful to thee for it, but I trust that it will be the last of the kind that we shall need to make ...

Purchased 1978, with the support of Jacqueline and Lewis Golden (through the Friends of the National Libraries) and the Victoria & Albert Museum Purchase Grant Fund

[22] *Priscilla Wordsworth, née Lloyd (d.1815)*

Portrait by John Constable (1776–1837)

December 1806   Pencil, 43.2 × 33.1 cm

Priscilla Lloyd married Christopher Wordsworth (1774–1846), the youngest
brother of the poet and the future Master of Trinity College, Cambridge,
in 1804. Priscilla's brother Charles and his wife, Sophia, lived at Brathay, and
were neighbours of John Harden of Brathay Hall, with whom Constable
was staying in 1806. Notice how Constable swings his right hand to shape
the hair and the shoulders of the figure; and, again, to deepen the shadow
to the right in order to highlight the silhouette.

Priscilla Wordsworth's papers are now with the Wordsworth Trust, her
diaries the gift of Priscilla Tolfree, 1990, and her letters the gift of Patrick
Tolfree, 2003. Both donors are descendents of Christopher and Priscilla
Wordsworth, and their son Christopher (1807–1885), who was Bishop of
Lincoln and Wordsworth's biographer.

*Purchased 1992, with the support of the MGC/V&A Purchase Grant Fund, the National Art
Collections Fund, Lloyds Bank and Sir Harry and Lady Djanogly*

[23] *William Wordsworth*

Portrait by Henry Edridge (1769–1821)

May 1806   Pencil and watercolour, 15.5 × 12.5 cm

This portrait was probably drawn in May 1806 while Wordsworth was a
guest of Sir George Beaumont in London. As a society painter, Edridge has
tidied up Wordsworth's strong features, producing the poet who would
have been at home in the drawing-rooms of Jane Austen. It was the nose
– rendered adequately Roman by Haydon (and less so by Chantrey, according to Hazlitt) – that had chiefly to be remodelled.

Eleanor Rawnsley Bequest, 1959

[24] *William Wordsworth*

The Thirteen-Book *Prelude*

1805   Manuscript

This is the first complete copy of Wordsworth's greatest single poetic achievement, the Thirteen-Book *Prelude*. It was made by Dorothy Wordsworth and later revised and corrected by her brother. The page illustrated here shows part of the description in Book XIII of Wordsworth's ascent of Snowdon:

> This small adventure, (for even such it seem'd
> In that wild place and at the dead of night)
> Being over and forgotten, on we wound
> In silence as before. With forehead bent
> Earthward, as if in opposition set
> Against an enemy, I panted up
> With eager pace, and no less eager thoughts.
>   a midnight
> Thus might we wear ~~perhaps an~~ hour away,
> Ascending at loose distance each from each,
> And I, as chanced, the foremost of the Band,
> When at my feet the ground appear'd to brighten,
> And with a step or two seem'd brighter still,
>   was   given to learn or
> Nor had I time to ask the cause of ~~this~~,
> For instantly a Light upon the turf
>   a startling gleam of startling power
> Fell like a flash: ~~I look'd about, and lo!~~
>   Yet mild and gentle; I lookd up—and lo
> The Moon stood naked in the Heavens, at height
>   Immense above my head, and on the shore
>   Of a huge sea, in clear and open air

Gordon Wordsworth Bequest, 1935

And, after ordinary Traveller's ~~chat~~ Talk
With our conductor, ~~silently~~ presently we ~~found~~
Each into commune with his private thoughts
~~Sunk~~ Thus did we breast the ascent ~~and~~ by myself
Was nothing either seen or heard the while
Which took me from my musings, save that once
The Shepherd's ~~cur~~ did to his own great joy
Unearth a hedge-hog in the mountain-crags
Round which he made a barking turbulent.
This small adventure, (for even such it seem'd
In that wild place and at the dead of night)
Being over and forgotten, on we wound
In silence as before. With forehead bent
Earthward, as if in opposition set
Against an enemy, I panted up
With eager pace and no less eager thoughts.
Thus might we wear ~~the~~ a midnight hour away,
Ascending at loose distance each from each,
And I, as chanced, the foremost of the Band,
When at my feet the ground appear'd to brighten,
And with a step or two seem'd brighter still;
Nor ~~had I time~~ was given to ~~seem~~ ~~or~~ ask the cause
For instantly a Light upon the turf
Fell like a flash; ~~I look'd~~ ~~about~~ ~~and lo~~
~~my eyes~~ and ~~lo~~ I look'd up = and lo
The Moon stood naked in the Heavens, at height
Immense above my head, and on the shore
Of a huge sea; in clear and open air

[25] *Sir George Beaumont (1753–1827)*

Peele Castle in a Storm

c. May 1806   Oil on canvas, 33.5 × 48.9 cm

Beaumont painted this subject twice, but it was this version that Wordsworth saw at Beaumont's house in Grosvenor Square in spring 1806. It
moved him to write his great *Elegaic Stanzas*, lamenting the death of his
brother John in a shipwreck off Weymouth Bay the previous year.

> Oh 'tis a passionate Work!—yet wise and well;
> Well chosen is the spirit that is here;
> That hulk which labours in the deadly swell,
> This rueful sky, this pageantry of fear!
>
> And this huge Castle, standing here sublime,
> I love to see the look with which it braves,
> Cased in the unfeeling armour of old time,
> The light'ning, the fierce wind, and trampling waves.
>
> Farewell, farewell the Heart that lives alone,
> Housed in a dream, at distance from the Kind!
> Such happiness, wherever it be known,
> Is to be pitied; for 'tis surely blind.
>
> But welcome fortitude, and patient chear,
> And frequent sights of what is to be borne!
> Such sights, or worse, as are before me here.—
> Not without hope we suffer and we mourn.

*Purchased 1993, with the support of the National Heritage Memorial Fund, the National Art
Collections Fund, the MGC/V&A Purchase Grant Fund, the Friends of the National Libraries,
the Binks Trust, the Clark Trust, Jared Curtis, Kenneth Ewing, John Harding, Kenneth Harris,
Frank Herrmann, Mary Lovell, the Sir George Martin Charitable Trust, Robert Pirie, Peter
Placito, Tom Stoppard, Oliver Turnbull and Delia Twamley*

[26] *Lady Beaumont (1756–1829)*

Portrait by Sir Joshua Reynolds

1788–9   Oil on canvas, 60 × 50 cm

This is one of two portraits of Lady Beaumont made by Joshua Reynolds from sittings in 1778 and March 1779, just after her marriage to Sir George Beaumont. With her husband, Lady Beaumont was the catalyst, part personal, part intellectual, for some of Wordsworth's finest work. It was she who encouraged Wordsworth to resume the writing of *The Prelude* after the death at sea of his brother John in 1805.

The Beaumonts met Wordsworth through their mutual friend Coleridge in 1803, and it was Coleridge who noted that Lady Beaumont had qualities which he had found in Dorothy Wordsworth: 'she verily has a soul in point of quick enthusiastic Feeling, most like to Dorothy's', he remarked. Lady Beaumont was also powerful at the dinner table, so much so that at times Sir George would have to apologise when she seemed to push Wordsworth's claims too far, and he humorously observed that his wife was as intolerant in her opinions as Bishop Bonner on religious matters.

Purchased 1996 from the Beaumont family, with the support of the National Heritage Memorial Fund and the Beecroft Bequest administered by the Museums Association

[27] *Sir George Beaumont (1753–1827)*

Peter Bell

1808   Oil on canvas, 34.6 × 42.5 cm

This painting is inscribed: 'suggested by the poem of Peter Bell by William Wordsworth not yet printed. After the close of the poem, Peter Bell is supposed to retire into a cavern, in which he continues stung with remorse and bewailing atrocities until day break. Painted by Sir George Beaumont at Coleorton in the year 1807.'

Wordsworth's poem *Peter Bell* was not published until 1819, but the first drafts belong to 1798. The idea that it should be published with an engraving based upon a picture by Beaumont was obviously the subject of discussion in 1808, and Beaumont, ever willing to support the poet's activities, first sent Wordsworth a pencil sketch. Wordsworth replied: 'I have no doubt that the picture will surpass it as far as the picture ought to do.' In the same letter Dorothy adds her comment on the painting (which, of course, she has not seen): 'I should think, independently of its connection with the poem, that the painting must gain very much by the change of time, from moonlight to early morning; and, as separating that scene entirely from the action contained in the poem, it is very judicious. There would have been some confusion if the moonlight had been preserved. I hope that the day will come when we shall see the picture itself, whether ever the poem be graced with an engraving from it or not.'

Purchased 1984 from the Beaumont family, with the support of the National Heritage Memorial Fund and the Victoria & Albert Museum Purchase Grant Fund

[28] *Joseph Wilkinson (1764–1831)*

Select Views in Cumberland, Westmoreland and Lancashire

London: for the Reverend Joseph Wilkinson, 1810

The anonymous introduction to Wilkinson's views is by Wordsworth. Wordsworth later revised and expanded this essay and published it as *A Topographical Description of the Country of the Lakes*, with the *River Duddon* sonnets in 1820. A third edition, again much revised, was published separately in 1822. The fifth edition of 1835, *A Guide through the District of the Lakes in the north of England*, was Wordsworth's final copy of this best-selling text, but further editions were published by Hudson of Kendal, with additional material for the benefit of tourists.

It is in the 1810 text that Wordsworth first makes his claim that 'persons of pure taste throughout the whole island, who, by, their visits (often repeated) to the Lakes in the North of England, testify that they deem the Lakes a sort of national property, in which every man has a right and interest who has a mind to perceive and a heart to enjoy'. Wordsworth's fear was that the new wealth would invade the 'district of the Lakes'. His book was written to ensure that 'a better taste should prevail among these new proprietors', so that there should be no 'unnecessary deviations from that path of simplicity and beauty along which, without design and unconsciously, their humble predecessors have moved'. Wordsworth was the first to state powerfully the need for an appropriate taste to be developed, in order that the Lake District could be preserved for its health-giving qualities. The idea of the National Park, not to be enacted until the 1960s, has its seeds in Wordsworth's thinking.

This is a presentation copy inscribed by Joseph Wilkinson on the front end-paper: 'William Wordsworth Esquire: from his faithful and obliged friend Joseph Wilkinson'. It contains Wordsworth's manuscript notes for the revised copy of the essay published in 1820.

Purchased 1996 from the estate of Margaret Goalby, with the support of the Friends of the National Libraries, Arco British Ltd, the Binks Trust, and the Roger and Sarah Bancroft Charitable Trust

SELECT VIEWS

IN

CUMBERLAND,

WESTMORELAND,

AND

LANCASHIRE.

BY THE REV. JOSEPH WILKINSON,

RECTOR OF EAST AND WEST WRETHAM, IN THE COUNTY OF NORFOLK,
AND CHAPLAIN TO

THE MARQUIS OF HUNTLY.

LONDON:

PUBLISHED, FOR THE REV. JOSEPH WILKINSON, BY R. ACKERMANN, AT HIS
REPOSITORY OF ARTS, 101, STRAND.

1810.

Harding and Bathe, Printers, 10 N. Strand.

[29] *William Wordsworth*

The Excursion Book IV and parts of Book I

Manuscript

The Prelude was not printed in Wordsworth's lifetime, but in 1814 he published *The Excursion*, the only other part of 'The Recluse' to be completed. Reception of the poem was mixed. Coleridge was disappointed. Francis Jeffrey began his attack in the *Edinburgh Review* with the words 'This will never do!' Blake was deeply offended by the Prospectus to 'The Recluse', published in the Preface. Byron was disparaging in *Don Juan*; and Leigh Hunt was so 'put out of sorts' by the poem that it made him uncomfortable to hear it mentioned in company, and his friends avoided the subject out of 'tenderness' for his feelings.

On the other hand, there were favourable and sensitive reviews of *The Excursion* from Lamb and Hazlitt. Shelley, though regretting Wordsworth's Establishment politics, borrowed from the poem; and Keats was strongly influenced. Benjamin Robert Haydon wrote opposite Book IV, lines 856–64, in his copy of the poem, 'Poor Keats used always to prefer this passage to all others':

> A distant strain far sweeter than the sounds
> Which his poor skill could make, his fancy fetched
> Even from the blazing chariot of the sun,
> A beardless youth, who touched a golden lute,
> And filled the illumined groves with ravishment.
> The nightly hunter, lifting up his eyes
> Towards the crescent moon with grateful heart,
> Called on the lovely wanderer who bestowed
> That timely light to share his joyous sport.

Gordon Graham Wordsworth Bequest, 1935

30

William Wordsworth

Portrait by Richard Carruthers (1792–1876)

1818   Oil on canvas , 73.7 × 61 cm

Wordsworth sat for this portrait in 1817. It was commissioned by Mary Wordsworth's cousin Thomas Monkhouse, who also had his own portrait painted. On 28 August 1817 Mary Wordsworth wrote that the poet had 'sate for his picture, written a few small poems, entertained company, enjoyed the country, and paid some visits and so his summer has been passed; he intends to work hard at the Recluse in Winter. … Wm's picture charming'.

Carruthers depicts Wordsworth with his head bowed onto his chest, a pose that is characteristic of later portraits by Pickersgill and Benjamin Robert Haydon [see no. 31]. It hung at Monkhouse's London residence where Haydon, a friend of his, would no doubt have seen it. It was also the first portrait of Wordsworth to be engraved (by Henry Meyer for the *New Monthly Magazine*, 1 February 1819) and as such was for many years the best-known image of the poet.

Soon after painting the portraits of Wordsworth and Monkhouse, Carruthers gave up art for business. 'He is an amiable young Man whom a favorable opening induced to sacrifice the Pencil to the Pen' Wordsworth told Francis Chantrey in October 1821, 'not the pen of Authorship—he is too wise for that—but the pen of the Counting House which he is success-fully driving at Lisbon'.

Gift of Joanna Hutchinson, 1957

31

William Wordsworth

Portrait by Benjamin Robert Haydon (1786–1846)

Inscribed: 'Wordsworth. For Entry into Jerusalem. 1819'
Pencil, 44.5 × 31.1 cm

This appears to be the full preparatory drawing Haydon made for the portrait of Wordsworth in his large oil, *Christ's Entry into Jerusalem*. It is also this drawing that was specifically praised by William Hazlitt in his essay *My First Acquaintance with Poets*, 1822:

> I think I see him now. He answered in some degree to his friend's description of him, but was more gaunt and Don Quixote-like. He was quaintly dressed (according to the costume of that unconstrained period) in a brown fustian jacket and striped pantaloons. There was something of a roll, a lounge in his gait, not unlike his own Peter Bell. There was a severe, worn pressure of thought about his temples, a fire in his eye (as if he saw something in objects more than the outward appearance), an intense high narrow forehead, a Roman nose, cheeks furrowed by strong purpose and feeling, and a convulsive inclination to laughter about the mouth, a good deal at variance with the solemn, stately expression of the rest of his face. Chantrey's bust wants the marking traits; but he was teazed into making it regular and heavy: Haydon's head of him, introduced into the Entrance of Christ into Jerusalem is the most like his drooping weight of thought and expression.

This portrait then is noted by Hazlitt, himself a painter and art critic, as the best likeness of Wordsworth that he knew. It is an impressive drawing; it had been missing for over a hundred years and is easily the most important portrait of Wordsworth to come to light.

Purchased 1993, with the support of the National Art Collections Fund, the National Heritage Memorial Fund, the MGC / V&A Purchase Grant Fund, Alan Bennett and Charles Warren

Wordsworth

For Ecoly with Servaticon
1825 —

[32] *William Wordsworth*

Ecclesiastical Sketches

Manuscript

This handmade notebook contains extensively revised drafts of twenty-three sonnets by William Wordsworth, afterwards published in *Ecclesiastical Sketches* (1822). Until its recent purchase, it was completely unknown to Wordsworth scholars. Up to now the only information on Wordsworth's process of composition of these important sonnets has been a transcript by one of Wordsworth's friends, John Kenyon. Kenyon was a conscientious transcriber, but his best efforts could not do full justice to the revisions and complexities of the original.

The sonnets give special emphasis to the role of the Church of England in the nineteenth century. Wordsworth tells how they came into being: 'During the month of December 1820 I accompanied a much-loved and honoured Friend in a walk through different parts of his Estate, with a view to fix upon the Site of a New Church which he intended to erect. It was one of the most beautiful mornings of a mild season, – our feelings were in harmony with the cherishing influences of the scene; and, such being our purpose, we were naturally led to look back upon past events with wonder and gratitude, and on the future with hope'. The friend was Sir George Beaumont, Wordsworth's friend and patron for twenty-five years.

Purchased 2000, with the support of the Heritage Lottery Fund and the W.W. Spooner Charitable Trust

Where liest thou green... in Albea that
                        was best
birth the first thus hers of Helvasued
What sin of Bard O might then...
                              can tele
Thy origa What Jena...   allest
Did help Paul, a wanderer in the
                              were
As some have taught, while in
And call thy soulean forth by... Breton chole
And in it dread signs thy rescued
                    us   Rretan two
Darkness surrounds, seeking we are
thick shade unpierceable of Onus
Marker that enrich the majesty where...
                                      y...
of Temples, shall governed in mountain
Entire, of seen in perfic... can the
Before ... ... to tune on earth
                              heaven.

[33] *Dora Wordsworth (1804–1847)*

Portrait by Margaret Gillies

1839   Watercolour on ivory, 19.4 × 12.1 cm

Margaret Gillies, who specialised in watercolour miniatures on ivory, requested a sitting from Wordsworth in the summer of 1839. She stayed at Rydal Mount for several weeks later that year and made portraits of the poet, Mary Wordsworth, Dora Wordsworth and Isabella Fenwick. The portrait of Dora Wordsworth was not immediately successful. 'Dora has been *attempted*,' Wordsworth wrote to Thomas Powell, 'but not yet, as we think, with much success.' On a visit to London Dora reported sitting again for Miss Gillies 'to have my nose reduced a little wh. she has done without at all injuring the original effect of her drawing.'

    Of all his children Wordsworth was most attached to Dora. This portrait was made when she was thirty-five years old, eighteen months before her marriage, on 11 May 1841, to Edward Quillinan, and eight years before her death.

Gift of Dorothy Dickson

[34] *Rotha Quillinan (1821–1876)*

Portrait by Sir William Boxall (1800–1879)

Dated 8 May 1832   Oil on canvas, 17 × 12.5 cm

Rotha was Wordsworth's godchild and the younger daughter of Edward Quillinan and his first wife Jemima (née Brydges), who died on 25 May 1822 as the result of a domestic fire. When Dora married Quillinan in 1841 Rotha became her godchild.

Attached behind this picture was a manuscript of Wordsworth's sonnet 'To Rotha Q——', published in 1827:

> Rotha, my Spiritual Child! this head was grey
> When at the sacred font for thee I stood;
> Pledged till thou reach the verge of womanhood,
> And shalt become thy own sufficient stay:
> Too late, I feel, sweet Orphan! was the day
> For stedfast hope the contract to fulfil;
> Yet shall my blessing hover o'er thee still,
> Embodied in the music of this Lay,
> Breathed forth beside the peaceful mountain Stream
> Whose murmur soothed thy languid Mother's ear
> After her throes, this Stream of name more dear
> Since thou dost bear it,—a memorial theme
> For others; for thy future self, a spell
> To summon fancies out of Time's dark cell.

The arist, Willliam Boxall, was the son of an Oxfordshire exciseman. He studied in the Royal Academy schools and in Italy. Wordsworth sat to him in London before 6 April 1831, when the poet dined with him and Edward Quillinan. He was appointed Director of the National Gallery in 1866.

Gift of the Higginbotham Woods family, 1999

William Wordsworth (1770–1850)

Portrait by Benjamin Robert Haydon

1843 . Oil on canvas, 91.4 × 71.1 cm

In 1840 Haydon sent Wordsworth an etching of his painting of his other great hero, the Duke of Wellington. In return Wordsworth sent a sonnet, which, he told Haydon, 'was actually composed while I was climbing Helvellyn'. Thus Wordsworth himself probably inspired Haydon to compose his famous portrait of the poet, deep in thought, on Helvellyn; this is now in the National Portrait Gallery, London.

This second portrait, also entitled *Wordsworth on Helvellyn*, shows the poet seated. Elizabeth Barrett, who had written a sonnet in praise of the earlier painting, wrote to Haydon:

> I like the new picture even better, in the general combination, than I did the last; although the head of the poet, probably from being less finished, is inferior as a likeness & expression of the individual intellect. But the general combination—the balancement of the scenic nature and the Humanity—is admirable—very grandly & suggestively preserved; the nature not stooping to the man, nor the man dwarfed before the nature—the wild sky & the serene forehead unabashed & unshrinking in the presence of each other. I like too that eagle in the cloud 'mewing his mighty strength' in sympathy with the poet-soul underneath him!—what am I that I should be gazing thus, from my sofa on eagles, & rocks & clouds?

The absence of an eagle would suggest that this painting is not the one that Elizabeth Barrett describes; but a description by Francis Bennoch, who once owned the seated Helvellyn portrait and was himself a friend of Haydon, makes it clear that the present canvas of 36 by 28 inches is only a portion of an original canvas 'about 4 or 5 feet square'. So at some point in the nineteenth century the painting was savagely cut.

Acquired 1927

THE AGE OF BRITISH ROMANTICISM

[36] *Samuel Taylor Coleridge (1772–1834)*

Verse Letter to Sara Hutchinson

1802   Manuscript

The first version of Coleridge's 'Dejection, An Ode' was written as a verse-letter to Sara Hutchinson on 4th April 1802. Coleridge had recently heard the four opening stanzas of Wordsworth's 'Immortality Ode'; he echoes and acknowledges that poem in his own, but asserts a grief that is far more bitter than Wordsworth's lament for the lost vision of childhood:

> A Grief without a pang, void, dark, & drear,
> A stifling, drowsy, unimpassion'd Grief
> That finds no natural outlet, no Relief,
> In word, or sigh, or tear—
> This, Sara! well thou know'st …

Though we can see that he was writing great poetry, Coleridge himself believed that his imagination had been stifled by the unhappiness of his marriage, and by isolation from the people he loved – Sara and the Wordsworths.

   This manuscript is one of two fair copies from a lost original. The second manuscript, in the hand of Mary Hutchinson, was purchased in 1978. A version of the poem, addressed to Wordsworth, was published in the *Morning Post* on Wordsworth's wedding day, 4 October 1802. Another even briefer version, stripped of biographical details, appeared in *Sybilline Leaves*, 1817, with the title 'Dejection: an ode'. The full confessional text was not published until 1937 (by Ernest de Selincourt), since when the publication of Coleridge's *Notebooks* and *Letters* have revealed the dark importance of Sara to Coleridge's creative and intellectual life.

Gordon Graham Wordsworth Bequest, 1935

A Letter to ————

April 4, 1802. —— Sunday Evening.

Well! if the Bard was weatherwise, who made
The grand old Ballad of Sir Patrick Spence,
This Night, so tranquil now, will not go hence
Unrous'd by winds, that ply a busier trade
Than that, which moulds yon clouds in lazy flakes,
Or the dull sobbing Draft, that drones & rakes
Upon the Strings of this Eolian Lute,
Which better far were mute.
For, lo! the ~~the~~ New Moon, winter-bright!
       overspread
And ~~overspread~~ with phantom Light,
(With swimming phantom Light o'erspread
But rimm'd & circled with a silver Thread)
I see the Old Moon in her Lap, foretelling
The coming-on of Rain & squally Blast———
O! Sara! that the Gust even now were swelling,
And the slant Night-shower driving loud &
                                        fast!

A Grief without a pang, void, dark, & drear,
A stifling, drowsy, unimpassion'd Grief
That finds no natural Outlet, no Relief
In word, or sigh, or tear ———
This, Sara! well thou knowst,

[37] *Samuel Taylor Coleridge*

Portrait by George Dance (1741–1825)

Dated 21 March 1804   Pencil, 16.2 × 19.8 cm

This portrait was probably commissioned by Sir George Beaumont, as was James Northcote's oil of Coleridge, made a few days later on 25–26 March. Coleridge, who was waiting in London to sail for the Mediterranean in search of a warmer climate and better health, had just suffered what he termed on the 20th 'a diarrhoea of incessant fury'. It was feared he might die abroad, and the portraits show the wish of his friend and admirer to preserve his likeness. Southey, however, when he saw Dance's portrait, could see no likeness at all: 'Dance's drawing has that merit at least', he wrote to Coleridge on 11 June, 'that nobody would ever suspect you of having been the original'.

Purchased 1984 from the Beaumont family, with the support of the National Heritage Memorial Fund and the Victoria & Albert Museum Purchase Grant Fund

Geo. Dance
March 21st 1804

[38] *Samuel Taylor Coleridge*

Portrait by James Northcote (1746–1831)

1804   Oil on canvas, 76.2 × 63.5 cm

There is a portrait similar to this one at Jesus College, Cambridge, though this may well be the original of the two. Robert Southey referred to one of them as showing Coleridge 'grinning', which is more likely to be this version. In June 1797 Dorothy Wordsworth had described Coleridge to Mary Hutchinson:

> He is a wonderful man ... he is pale and thin, has a wide mouth, thick lips and not very good teeth, longish, loose-growing half-curling rough black hair. But if you hear him speak for five minutes you think no more of them. His eye is large and full, not dark but grey; such an eye as would receive from a heavy soul the dullest expression; but it speaks every emotion of his animated mind; it has more of the 'poet's eye in fine frenzy rolling' than I ever witnessed. He has fine dark eyebrows, and an overhanging forehead.

The subsequent change in his physical appearance, the result of ill-health and opium addiction, is evident in this portrait. De Quincey wrote:

> Coleridge's face, as is well known to his acquaintances, exposed a large surface of cheek; too large for the intellectual expression of his features generally, had not the final effect been redeemed by what Wordsworth styled his 'godlike forehead.' The result was that no possible face so broadly betrayed and published any effects whatever, especially these lustrous effects from excesses in opium. For some years I failed to consider reflectively, or else, reflecting, I failed to decipher, this resplendent acreage of cheek. But at last, either *proprio marte*, or prompted by some medical hint, I came to understand that the glistening face, glorious from afar like the old Pagan face of the demigod Æsculapius, simply reported the gathering accumulation of insensible perspiration.

Purchased 1986, with the support of the MGC/V&A Purchase Grant Fund

39

Charles Lloyd (1775–1839)

Poems on the Death of Priscilla Farmer

Bristol: N. Biggs, 1796

This very rare folio includes Coleridge's sonnet 'The piteous sobs that choke the virgin's breath', and Charles Lamb's 'Grandam', both of which, along with all but one of Lloyd's poems here, were reprinted in the second edition of Coleridge's *Poems*, 1797.

In 1796 Lloyd went to live with the Coleridges at Nether Stowey. The arrangement was that he would receive board, lodging and tuition for £80 a year. Three years younger than Coleridge, he had recently given up his job at the bank and turned poet, publishing *Poems on Various Subjects* in 1795. 'Charles Lloyd wins upon me hourly', Coleridge wrote to Thomas Poole, 'his heart is uncommonly pure, his affections delicate, & his benevolence enlivened, but not sicklied, by sensibility.—He is assuredly a man of great Genius; but it must be in tête-à-tête with one whom he loves & esteems, that his colloquial power open'.

Priscilla Farmer was Charles Lloyd's grandmother; her daughter married Charles Lloyd the Quaker and co-founder of the bank. 'I can but notice', Charles Lamb wrote when he received this volume, 'the odd coincidence of two young men, in one age, carolling their grandmothers', adding, 'I cannot but smile to see my granny so daily decked forth.'

The publication of *Edmund Oliver* in 1798, a novel in which Lloyd drew upon details of Coleridge's early life, seemed to Coleridge a betrayal. Though Lloyd married and came to live at Brathay near Ambleside, neither Coleridge nor Wordsworth, though still acquainted with him, allowed the friendship to be continued.

The Geoffrey Bindman Collection, purchased in 2004 with the support of the Heritage Lottery Fund, the J. Paul Getty Jr Charitable Trust, the Friends of the National Libraries, Sir Harry and Lady Djanogly, the Charles Warren Bequest, the Roger and Sarah Bancroft Charitable Trust, the Chris Brasher Trust, John and Sally Barker, John Dobson, and other private donors

P O E M S

ON

The Death

OF

P R I S C I L L A   F A R M E R,

BY HER GRANDSON

CHARLES LLOYD.

DEATH! THOU HAST VISITED THAT PLEASANT PLACE,
WHERE IN THIS HARD WORLD I HAVE HAPPIEST BEEN.

BOWLES.

BRISTOL:
PRINTED BY N. BIGGS,
And Sold by JAMES PHILLIPS, George-Yard, Lombard-Street, LONDON.

1796.

40

Samuel Taylor Coleridge

Portrait by Washington Allston (1779–1843)

1814   Oil on canvas, 114.3 × 87.6 cm

Washington Allston, an American, became a friend of Coleridge in Rome late in 1805. Hearing of the peace between the French and the Austrians, and fearing that he might be marked for Napoleon's special animosity because of anti-French newspaper articles he had published between 1800 and 1803, Coleridge went to Allston's house at Olevano Romano, thirty miles from Rome. An immediate and lasting sympathy sprang up between the two men. Coleridge left Italy in May 1806; three years later, Allston returned to America, married a sister of W. E. Channing, and came with her on his second visit to London in 1811. He then went to Bristol, apparently for his health, and there he painted this portrait. It was done for Josiah Wade, an accountant and Bristol friend of Coleridge with whom the poet often stayed.

In the portrait the face points slightly upwards; the head dominates from its position and from its colouring, which is rich and warm; the idea of aspiration is continued by a formal Gothic window on the left; beside the window is a dark niche from which an antique statue looks out (but in an opposite direction from Coleridge himself) towards a dim, suffused light. In his left hand Coleridge holds a small, closed book, which in brightness is second only to the face. In contrast to the domestic portrait Allston sketched of Coleridge in Rome in 1806 this is deliberately heroic: a reverential statement of Coleridge's intellectual power. 'To no other man whom I have known, do I owe so much intellectually as to Mr. Coleridge', Allston wrote to a friend, 'when I recall some of our walks under the pines of the Villa Borghese. I am almost tempted to dream that I once listened to Plato, in the groves of the Academy.'

On long-term loan from the National Portrait Gallery, London

[41] *Hartley Coleridge (1796–1849)*

Portrait by Sir David Wilkie (1745–1841)

1806   Oil on canvas, 22 × 18 cm

Coleridge's son Hartley was ten years old when this portrait was made.
'Hartley is what he always was', Coleridge had written three years earlier, 'a
strange strange Boy—"*exquisitely wild*"! An utter Visionary! like the Moon
among thin Clouds, he moves in a circle of Light of his own making—he
alone, in a Light of his own. Of all human Beings I never yet saw one so
utterly naked of *Self*—he has no Vanity, no Pride, no Resentment, and tho'
very passionate, I have never yet seen him *angry with* any body.' Wordsworth,
as well as Coleridge, wondered at Hartley's gifts; this extract is from
Wordsworth's, 'To H.C., Six Years Old':

> O Thou! whose fancies from afar are brought;
> Who of thy words dost make a mock apparel,
> And fittest to unutterable thought
> The breeze-like motion and the self-born carol;
> Thou Faery Voyager! that dost float
> In such clear water, that thy Boat
> May rather seem
> To brood on air than on an earthly stream;
> Suspended in a stream as clear as sky,
> Where earth and heaven do make one imagery;
> O blessed Vision! happy Child!
> Thou art so exquisitely wild,
> I think of thee with many fears
> For what may be thy lot in future years.

Hartley published a much praised collection, *Poems*, in 1833, but in general
did not live up to his promise. He lost his Oxford fellowship through intem-
perance, worked unsuccessfully as a schoolmaster, and spent most of his
later life in the Lake District.

*Purchased 1984 from the Beaumont family, with the support of the National Heritage Memorial
Fund and the Victoria & Albert Museum Purchase Grant Fund*

[42] *Robert Southey (1774–1843)*

Portrait by Thomas Phillips (1770–1845)

*c.*1818   Oil on canvas, 90 × 70 cm

The original drawing for this portrait, commissioned by the publisher John Murray, was completed by November 1815, when Southey wrote to Mary Barker, 9 November 1815: 'The devil who owes me an old grudge has made me sit to Phillips for a picture for Murray.' Southey liked to grumble about the pains of being famous – after he became Poet Laureate. The mezzotint derived from the painting he declared to be 'bad, base, vile, vulgar, odious, hateful, detestable, abominable, execrable, and infamous. The rascally mezzotint scraper has made my face fat, fleshy, silly and sensual, and given the eyes an expression which I conceive to be more like two oysters in love than anything else'

  Southey was a major literary figure, not least in his prose, who comes into the lives of Coleridge, Wordsworth, Shelley, Byron, and many, many others. He is a figure whose work is intimately bound up with that of his contemporaries. In 1831 John Stuart Mill called him 'a mild man with bitter opinions'; Queen Victoria knew of him as the author of the *Life of Nelson*; Lewis Carroll, irreverently, found him to be a poet eminently worthy of mockery (in 'You are old, Father William'); Byron found in him the obstinate reactionary force against which he turned all his fierce satire. He was the mocked dedicatee of his *Don Juan*, 1818, and the bumbling and overweening poet in his most succinct attack: 'The Vision of Judgment', published in *The Liberal*, 1822.

Purchased 1994, with the support of the MGC/V&A Purchase Grant Fund and the National Art Collections Fund. Conserved with the generous assistance of the North West Museums Service

[43] *Caroline Bowles (1786–1854)*

Robert Southey's Study at Greta Hall

February 1841   Watercolour, 43.4 × 35.6 cm

Southey was deeply committed to the reading and writing of books. One of his most significant poems is entitled 'My days among the Dead are past', and is a reference to his literary interests:

> My days among the Dead are past;
>   Around me I behold,
> Where'er these casual eyes are cast,
>   The mighty minds of old;
> My never failing friends are they,
> With whom I converse day by day …
>
> My hopes are with the dead, anon
>   My place with them will be,
> And I with them shall travel on
>   Through all Futurity;
> Yet leaving here a name, I trust,
> That will not perish in the dust.

The purchase of books was Southey's one clear extravangance. On his death his library at Greta Hall held some 14,000 volumes. When Percy Bysshe Shelley visited Southey at Keswick in 1811–12, he found that he was permitted into Southey's study, but forbidden to take down the books from their shelves. He concluded that this was because Southey considered their riches to be secret, and for himself alone.

The view is towards St John's, the new church, with the market hall to the right in the middle window. The hill behind is Walla Crag.

The Greta Hall Collection, purchased with the support of the Heritage Lottery Fund and the Lake Poets Society, 2003

[44] *Charles Lamb (1775–1834) and Mary Lamb (1764–1847)*

Portrait by Francis Cary (1808–1880)

1834   Oil on canvas, 113 × 85.1 cm

To Wordsworth, writing about Lamb after his death, he was 'the frolic and the gentle'. To Coleridge, a lifelong friend from their days together at Christ's Hospital school, he was 'my gentle-hearted Charles'. The public knew him as a fine essayist, a sympathetic critic, and an occasional poet. His first real literary success was the collection of prose adaptations of Shakespeare for children, *Tales from Shakespeare,* 1807; he wrote the tragedies, his sister Mary the comedies and histories. His collected miscellaneous writings were published in 1818, and between 1820 and 1823, he was a regular contributor to the *London Magazine,* writing a series of popular essays under the name 'Elia'. The collected *Essays of Elia* were published in 1823 and 1833. 'Mr Lamb has succeeded not by comforming to the *Spirit of the Age,*' wrote William Hazlitt in 1825, 'but in opposition to it. He does not march boldly along with the crowd, but steals off the pavement to pick his way in the contrary direction. He prefers *bye-ways* to *highways.*'

The artist of this moving portrait was the son of the great Dante translator, Henry Cary. It shows Charles and Mary Lamb in old age, and is the only known image of Mary Lamb. The picture is not quite completed, for Charles Lamb died while it was being painted. It is appropriate that brother and sister should appear together, for after Mary had murdered her mother in a fit of madness in 1799, Charles was her devoted keeper. Emma Moxon, their godchild, who knew the Lambs intimately, wrote to Cary: 'I am sure anyone who at all knew them would at once see how exactly you have pictured them.'

On long-term loan from the National Portrait Gallery, London

[45] *John Wilson (1785–1854)*

Portrait by Sir Henry Raeburn (1756–1823)

Oil on canvas, 236 × 149.3 cm

Wilson is an example of one several young writers who were attracted to the Lake District by the presence of Wordsworth. He first came to Elleray on Windermere aged twenty-one, probably accompanied by Alexander Nasmyth the Scottish painter. By 3 October 1805 he had bought ground with a cottage below Orrest Head (and now found on the side of the road opposite to Windermere railway station).

Wilson in these early years was wealthy enough to enjoy the sports of fishing and wrestling and to indulge in literary pursuits. When he became editor of *Blackwoods Magazine* in 1819 his inherited wealth was disappearing and he had to earn his living by his journalism. He wrote under the signature 'Christopher North', and his criticism could be savage – reviewing Coleridge's *Biographia Literaria* he called the author 'both a wicked and pernicious member of society', and with John Gibson Lockhart he violently attacked the so-called 'Cockney' poets Leigh Hunt and John Keats. He was, however, an early champion of Shelley's poetry, and considered Wordsworth, Walter Scott and Byron to be 'the great master-spirits of our day'. In 1820 Wilson further supplemented his income by becoming Professor of Moral Philosophy at the University of Edinburgh.

Henry Raeburn was one of the most successful Scottish painters of the time. Extremely prolific, his portraits form a remarkable visual record of Scottish society in the late eighteenth and early nineteenth centuries. Here, he shows Wilson aged seventeen, the age when, still at school, Wilson wrote an admiring letter to Wordsworth. To Wilson's one criticism, that Wordsworth chose unsuitable subjects (such as 'The Idiot Boy'), Wordsworth replied that a poet 'ought to travel before men occasionally as well as at their sides'.

On long-term loan from the Scottish National Portrait Gallery

[46] *Thomas De Quincey (1785–1859)*

Letter to John Wordsworth

28 March 1809   Manuscript

De Quincey's great delight in children is best illustrated by his letters to Johnny, Wordsworth's eldest son. In this letter he takes the trouble to print the letters so that the boy might read them. He tells him about his brother Richard, a sailor, who is depicted as a hero and adventurer.

Earlier that month Dorothy Wordsworth had told De Quincey: 'When your Friend Johnny came from school last night, his mother said to him, "Here is a letter *from* ——." "From," he replied, "Mr. De Quincey?" And with his own ingenuous blush and smile he came forward to the fireside at a quicker pace, and asked me to read the letter; which I did, with a few omissions and levelling the language to his capacity, and you would have thought yourself well repaid for the trouble of writing it if you could only have seen how feelingly he was interested. When it was all over, he says "but when will he come? Maybe he'll tell us in his next letter." We hope that before you return he will be much improved in his reading, for he seems now to desire to learn and takes a great deal of notice not only of his own lessons but of the lessons of the bigger Boys.'

'My dear Friend', De Quincey begins,

> Ever since your Aunt Dorothy told me that you could read I have been intending to print a letter to you—both because I promised that I would—and also because I thought that you would like it. But perhaps you will not like a very long one, therefore I shall make it a very middling sized one.
>
> As soon as I come to live at Grasmere, I shall begin to teach you all the things which I know that I think you would like to know: one thing will be Swimming: another will be how to fly a kite: and another will be swinging: and another walking on stilts. But the best thing of all will be how to sail in a boat upon the lake …

Gordon Graham Wordsworth Bequest, 1935

soon for my letter to Johnny. I shall be at Grasmere certainly within a day or two after ~~the~~ this letter; for I shall travel home at once, when I once set off; and that will be ~~I hope~~ to-morrow. — Give my kindest love to Miss Wordsworth and Miss Hutchin
-n — and remain, my dear Madam, with the greatest affection and respect, your faithful friend and servant, W: de Quincey"

My dear Friend, Ever since your Aunt Dorothy told me that your could read, I have been intending to print a letter to you——both because I promised that I would—and also because I thought that you would like it. But perhaps ~~you~~ you will not like a very long one; there-fore I shall make it only a middling sized one.

As soon as I come to live at Grasmere, I shall begin to teach you all the things which I know that I think you would like to know: one thing will be Swimming: another will be how to fly a kite: and another will be swinging: and another walking on Stilts. But the best thing of all will be how to sail in a boat upon the lake—and to make the boat go which way you like—both when it has a sail and when it has not one. But it is not I that am to teach you this——but it is my Brother—who is a sailor. He has promised to come and teach both your and me all about Ships and Boats—both how to sail them and how to make them; for he can make boats.

And besides teaching us these things, my Brother can tell us a great many stories that are really. For he has been sailing all round the world ever since the time when were a little Baby as little as Catherine. He has been in cold Countries—where there is no day-light for many many weeks. He has been amongst great Forests where there are were only Lions and Bears and Wolves— And amongst many nations of Black men and men that are the color of copper. He has also been past the country where Giants live: they are called Pata-gonians. He has been in Battles—and has seen great Towns ~~burning~~: and sometimes, the men that he fought against caught him and put him in prison. He Once he was in that Island where Robinson Crusoe and his man Friday lived: I dare say your Mother or your Aunt has told you about them.

One of the Stories that he told me is a short story: therefore I shall print it here. One time when my Brother was sailing near Africa in an English Ship that was called ___: there were about one hundred more men with him in the Ship. First as the ___ was going down, they saw another Ship that was sailing towards em. Soon ___ came close to them; then the men in my Brother's Ship said "Where do you come from? — The people in the other Ship said We ___ Them Spain — We are Spaniards. So then because the Spaniards were not the Friends of the English at that time as they are now. ~~these two~~ there was a Battle between these Ships in the dark night. And the English Ship beat the Spanish Ship. Then the Captain of the English Ship said to my Brother and to some other en You must go into that Spanish Ship and put Chains upon all the Spaniards that are not dead and then make the Ship follow this Ship. So my Brother and thirty ther men went and did as the Captain told them to do They put chains upon the

[47] *Thomas De Quincey*

Portrait by James Archer (1823–1904)

1855   Chalk, 52.5 × 56.5 cm

Thomas De Quincey is here shown with his daughters Emily and Margaret, and his granddaughter Eva Craig. This is one of three drawings of the De Quincey family done by James Archer, a Scottish painter of genre portraits, landscapes and medieval historical scenes. The others are a group portrait of Emily, Florence and Margaret De Quincey, and a pastel of Florence, both dated 1853. The Trust has also recently acquired a set of miniatures that are clearly derived from these portraits. A posthumous oil of De Quincey by Archer is in Manchester City Art Gallery.

De Quincey's daughters were an increasing support to their father in the last twenty years of his life, largely spent at Lasswade, near Edinburgh. Florence De Quincey became Mrs Baird Smith, and was one of the earliest supporters of the Wordsworth Trust when it was set up in 1891.

Purchased 2005 from Eric De Quincey with the support of the Art Fund, the MLA/V&A Purchase Grant Fund, Piet de Jong and the W.W. Spooner Charitable Trust

[48] *Thomas De Quincey*

Confessions of an English Opium Eater

1821   Manuscript

Written in his London lodgings, 4 York Street (now Tavistock Street), Covent Garden, in 1821. The *Confessions* is not only remarkable for its treatment of the then obscure predicament of those who are addicted to opium; it is also a dark testament to the wondrous qualities and powers of the human mind. While Wordsworth saw the mind as the centre of the imagination and a redeeming force, for De Quincey it was an instrument that could approach the world of madness. It was De Quincey's good fortune that he was the only one of the younger writers of the Romantic period who had read Wordsworth's *Prelude* (in manuscript), and therefore he was able to draw upon the older poet's marvellous technique of presenting 'spots of time', those significant memories which revivify a person's life throughout its course.

This manuscript was formerly in the possession of Lord Rosebery, Prime Minister 1894–5. The text was first published in the *London Magazine* and the editorial changes are in the hand of its editor, John Taylor. The manuscript of the second article has not survived.

Purchased 1988, with the support of the National Heritage Memorial Fund, the Pilgrim Trust, the Esmée Fairbairn Foundation, Philip Robinson, Arthur Andersen Ltd, and other private donors

Confessions of an English Opium-Eater.
[Being an Extract from the Life of a Scholar].

To the ~~Editor~~ ~~London~~ Reader.

I have presented you, courteous Reader, with the record of a remarkable period in my own life: according to my application of it, ~~for the purposes which I shall~~ ~~now point out, may be~~ ~~the benefit of a numerous class of persons.~~ I trust that it will prove not merely an interesting record but in a considerable degree useful and instructive ¿. In that hope it is that I have drawn it up: and that must be my apology for the breaking through those delicate restraints of ~~pride and~~ ~~delicacy and humility~~ ~~[honourable pride]~~ which for the most part impose silence on all ~~voluntary~~ ~~to the public eye of~~ public exposures of a ~~it~~ human ~~history~~ errors and infirmities. Nothing indeed is more revolting to English feelings [the spectacle of] ~~than for a human being coarsely obtruding upon their notice~~ his moral ulcers ~~and~~ or scars — ~~voluntary~~ and tearing away that "decent drapery" which time or indulgence to human frailty may have drawn over them: accordingly the greater part of our ~~English~~ ~~judicial~~ confessions ~~running~~ that is spontaneous and extra-judicial confessions proceed from ~~Convicts~~ ~~[any such act of gratuitous self-revelation]~~ adventurers, or Swindlers: and for ~~the commiseration which such confessions may be supposed~~ he can be supposed in sympathy with the decent and self-respecting part of Society we must look ~~elsewhere~~ to French Literature, or to that part of the German which is tainted with the luxurious and defective sensibility of the French. All this I feel so forcibly, and so nervously am I alive to reproach of this tendency, that I have for many months hesitated about the propriety of

[49] *William Hazlitt (1778–1830)*

Portrait by William Bewick (1795–1866)

1824   Chalk, 48 × 33.5 cm

When Hazlitt ran his series of *Lectures on the English Poets* between January and March 1818, William Bewick made a point of attending – 'He is the Shakespeare prose writer of our glorious country', he wrote to his brother, 'he outdoes all in truth, style, and originality'. An intimate friendship developed, and to Bewick's admiration for Hazlitt's intellect was added an artist's fascination with the oddities of his personality and manner – 'in his intellectual strength, his frailties, and his inequalities,' he recalled, 'William Hazlitt was indeed an enigma and a riddle'.

Bewick made this vivid portrait after a pleasant day's walking and fishing in Scotland (where Hazlitt was awaiting his divorce from Sarah Stoddart), and it pleased the sitter so much that he had Bewick prop it on the mantelpiece with a couple of forks so that he might look at it over his dinner. Bewick later recalled:

> He frequently laid down his knife and fork to contemplate the likeness, gazing earnestly and long, asking if really his own hair was anything like that of the drawing. Mrs. Hazlitt exclaimed, 'Oh! it is exactly your own hair, my dear.' With which he seemed quite satisfied, and in great admiration of what I had done, said, 'Well, surely that puts me in mind of some of Raphael's heads in the cartoons. Ah! it is, however, something to live for, to have such a head as that.' He contemplated the representation of himself for some time in silence, with evident expressions of satisfaction, not unmixed with some natural emotion of vanity, which in him was neutralised by the genuine simplicity of his character.

There are two other versions of this portrait – at the National Portrait Gallery, London, and Maidstone Museum.

Gift of Mrs. J. V. Dundas Lemont, 1990

[50] *William Hazlitt (1778–1830)*

On Egotism

*c.*1826   Manuscript

This is a rare example of one of Hazlitt's working manuscripts, a fragment
of his essay 'On Egotism', published in 1826 as part of *The Plain Speaker:
Opinions on Books, Men and Things.*

> Let any one be brought up among books, and taught to think words the
> only things, and he may conceive highly of himself from the proficiency
> he has made in language and in letters. Let him then be compelled to at-
> tempt some other pursuit—painting, for instance—and be made to feel
> the difficulties, the refinements of which it is capable, and the number
> of things of which he was utterly ignorant before, and there will be an
> end of his pedantry and his pride together.

The manuscript is inscribed, possibly by Hazlitt's son William Carew
Hazlitt: 'Manuscript of William Hazlitt / Given by son William Hazlitt / to
Jabez Hogg / 11 August 1850'.

Gift of Michael Foot, 1998

"I was only going to say, my Lord," said Evan in what he meant to be an insinuating manner, "that if your gallant honour and the honourable gentlemen would let Vich Ian Vohr go free just this once & let him gae back to France & not trouble King George ye ſeldom again and that he ſall promiſe never to come back again, & if you'll just tell me gae willing to be hanged in his stead; & if you'll just tell me gae soon as Glen required, I'll fetch them up to ye myself to be ... and on large figure was begun with one ... past man ..

... ...

This is Highland Reports; but still ... these &c. all these ... ... Make, it to time until ... I can only ... believe of or what is actually done. —

Their conduct is as much affected by the ... of this as if they actually ... by the ... Hampshire that they repented ... new murders ... upon our murders whilst not having any fancy or opinion the ... upon our murder whilst not having ... But as ... the ... ... be allowed with the others. But are ... ... itself. Being more ... ... a ... physical ... or one or more ... but does it ... partly ... causes me to have an ... ... whilst adds a ... to the number of ... ... disturbed in ... ... & having ... ... all ... our ... feelings

Thomas Moore (1779–1852)

The Fudge Family in Paris

London: Longman, Hurst, Rees, Orme and Brown, 1818

This copy of Thomas Moore's *The Fudge Family in Paris* (a third edition) has led to scholarly debates. It is inscribed 'To William Hazlitt Esqr as a small mark of respect for his literary talents & political principles from the author. April 27th , 1818'. According to Buxton Forman, the volume came into the possession of P.P. Howe in October 1934. Hyder Rollins in his *Keats Letters* (Harvard, 1958) is unable to accept that in one of Keats' great letters, to John Hamilton Reynolds, 3 May 1818, the favourable reference to 'Moore's present' is in fact to this volume. Keats' words are: 'After all there is certainly something real in the World – Moore's present to Hazlitt is real – I like that Moore, and am glad that I saw him at the theatre just before I left town.'

Rollins suggests that 'Hazlitt disliked and disparaged Moore'. Hazlitt certainly did by the time he came to write *The Spirit of the Age*, 1825, but not in 1818 or 1819. Hazlitt's discussion of Sheridan in Lecture VII of his *Lectures on the English Comic Writers*, 1819, was reported in the *Morning Chronicle*, 8 January 1819, to Moore's great pleasure. Moore in his diary on 9 January 1819 notes with satisfaction: 'Hazlitt's lecture on Sheridan (quoted in the Chronicle of this morning, and containing a warm eulogium on me) led us to talk on humour'. Moore was clearly pleased, and Hazlitt's allusion to Moore's undertaking the *Life of Sheridan* shows the then warmth of Hazlitt's affection:

> His character will, however, soon be drawn by one who has all the abil-
> ity, and every inclination to do him justice; who knows how to bestow
> praise and how to deserve it; by one who himself is an ornament of pri-
> vate and public life; a satirist, beloved by his friends; a wit and a patriot
> to-boot; a poet, and an honest man.

Gift of Michael Foot, 2004

THE

FUDGE FAMILY

IN

Paris.

EDITED BY

THOMAS BROWN, THE YOUNGER,

AUTHOR OF THE TWOPENNY POST-BAG.

Le Leggi della Maschera richiedono che una persona masche-
rata non sia salutata per nome da uno che la conosce malgrado il
suo travestimento.—CASTIGLIONE.

THIRD EDITION.

LONDON:

PRINTED FOR LONGMAN, HURST, REES, ORME,
AND BROWN, PATERNOSTER-ROW.

1818.

[52] *William Godwin (1756–1836)*

Portrait by Francis Chandler (*c.*1770–1804/5)

1798   Oil on canvas, 64.9 × 62.2 cm

William Godwin was arguably, in the early manhood of Wordsworth and Coleridge, the most famous of English writers. In his two volume *Political Justice* (1793), Godwin based his radicalism on an optimistic belief in human reason, as a means to dipense with authoritarian controls and governmental machinery. Naturally reform could not be based on anything as unreasonable as violence: for him the French Revolution was not the model.

Godwin was also a novelist. His *Caleb Williams*, 1794 suggests that the oppression of the hero Caleb derived from the organisation of society: his subtitle, 'Things As They Are', indicates that Godwin's purpose was to analyse and demonstrate the faults of contemporary society.

In *Political Justice* Godwin argued against the institution of marriage but he was to contradict his theories when in 1797 he married the pregnant Mary Wollstonecraft, whose *Vindication of the Rights of Woman* (1792) established her as the first British feminist. Mary died in childbirth in September 1797 and Godwin was left with two children, Mary's daughter Fanny Imlay and the infant Mary. His marriage to Mary Jane Clairmont in 1803 emphatically domesticated him, for she, a widow, already had two children; a fifth child William, was born to them in 1805. Godwin needed money and enterprisingly published a series of children's books with his new wife. Among their authors were Charles and Mary Lamb.

This fine portrait was made shortly after his wife's death.

On long-term loan from the Tate Gallery, London

[53] *William Godwin*

An Enquiry Concerning Political Justice

London: G. G. J. and J.Robinson, 1792

In February 1793, the year of its publication, Godwin contrived to send a copy of *Political Justice* to the National Convention in Paris by way of a friend, John Fenwick. Against the backdrop of an increasingly violent French revolution, the book put forward an essentially optimistic philosophy: 'the human mind in every enlightened age is progressive' Godwin writes in the preface, and then later: 'Man is perfectible, or in other words susceptible of perpetual improvement.' Perfection, he argues, can be arrived at through the power of human reason, which throughout history has been hindered by the 'brute engine' of political government, and by artificial social institutions such as marriage:

> The institution of marriage is a system of fraud; and men who carefully mislead their judgements in the daily affair of their life, must always have a crippled judgement in every other concern ... Add to this, that marriage is an affair of property, and the worst of all properties ... So long as I seek to engross one woman to myself, and to prohibit my neighbour from proving his superior desert and reaping the fruits of it, I am guilty of the most odious of all monopolies.

Godwin later defended his marriage to Mary Wollstonecraft by arguing that it was not 'an affair of property', but a neccessary compliance to public opinion: 'I find the prejudice of the world in arms against the woman who practically opposes herself to the European institution of marriage. I found that the comfort and peace of a woman for whose comfort and peace I interest myself would be much injured if I could have prevailed on her to defy those prejudices.'

The Geoffrey Bindman Collection, purchased in 2004 with the support of the Heritage Lottery Fund, the J. Paul Getty Jr Charitable Trust, the Friends of the National Libraries, Sir Harry and Lady Djanogly, the Charles Warren Bequest, the Roger and Sarah Bancroft Charitable Trust, the Chris Brasher Trust, John and Sally Barker, John Dobson, and other private donors

AN

E N Q U I R Y

CONCERNING

POLITICAL JUSTICE,

AND

ITS INFLUENCE

ON

GENERAL VIRTUE AND HAPPINESS.

BY

WILLIAM GODWIN.

IN TWO VOLUMES,

VOL. I.

LONDON:

PRINTED FOR G. G. J. AND J. ROBINSON, PATERNOSTER-ROW.

M.DCC.XCIII.

[54] *Mary Wollstonecraft (1759–1792)*

A Vindication of the Rights of Woman

London: Joseph Johnson, 1792

This is Mary Wollstonecraft's most famous work, and deservedly so, for the sheer force and originality of the thinking behind it. It was written in the last months of 1791, when she was living in Store Street, behind the British Museum. Although she never said so, it is at least possible she had some encouragement from Thomas Paine, a close friend of the French philosopher Condorcet, who had already written advocating equal rights for women in his *Lettres d'un bourgeois de Newhaven* in 1787 and again in *Sur l'admission des femmes au droit de cité* in 1790.

Her argument is that mind has no sex; that if women were educated in the same way as men they would perform as well; and that society was wasting its assets by failing to educate them and offer them the opportunity to work in the same areas as men, and to be economically independent: 'is not that Government ... very defective, and very unmindful of the happiness of one half of its members, that does not provide for honest, independent women, by encouraging them to fill respectable stations?' Men are as much corrupted by being tyrants as women by being subject to them, she pointed out. They 'may be convenient slaves, but slavery will have its constant effect, degrading the master and the abject dependent.'

Marriage was often no more than 'legal prostitution' under such a system. Prostitutes were ignorant and unfortunate rather than wicked, and not helped by asylums: 'It is justice, not charity, that is wanting in the world!' Women should be trained for the professions and could run businesses and farms. She raised the question of suffrage, but deferred it to a further volume, pointing out meanwhile that large numbers of working men were also without the vote and forced to 'pay for the support of royalty when they can scarcely stop their children's mouths with bread'.

Purhased with the assistance of the John Finch Memorial Fund

A

VINDICATION

OF THE

RIGHTS OF WOMAN:

WITH

STRICTURES

ON

POLITICAL AND MORAL SUBJECTS.

By MARY WOLLSTONECRAFT.

VOL. I.
THE SECOND EDITION.

LONDON:

PRINTED FOR J. JOHNSON, N° 72, ST. PAUL'S CHURCH YARD.

1792.

[55] *Joseph Severn (1793–1879)*

Shelley Composing *Prometheus Unbound* in the Baths of Caracalla

1845   Oil on canvas, 99.1 × 124.8 cm

This painting was commissioned by the Shelleys' son, Percy Florence. Severn based the figure of Shelley on Amelia Curran's portrait, which Mary Shelley had lent him. The Baths of Caracalla was one the poet's favourite spots in Rome, where he lived in 1819. In his preface to *Prometheus Unbound* he wrote:

> This Poem was chiefly written upon the mountainous ruins of the Baths of Caracalla, among the flowery glades, and thickets of odiferous blossoming trees, which are extending in ever-winding labyrinths upon its immense platforms and dizzy arches suspended in the air. The bright blue sky of Rome, and the effect of the vigorous awakening of spring in that divinest climate, and the new life with which it drenches the spirits even to intoxication, were the inspiration of this drama.

Severn and Shelley never met, but Shelley had praised Severn in the preface to *Adonais* for his devoted attention to Keats during the poet's last days in Rome: 'Mr. Severn can dispense with a reward from "such stuff as dreams are made of." His conduct is a golden augury of the success of his future career—may the unextinguished Spirit of his illustrious friend animate the creations of his pencil, and plead against Oblivion for his name.'
    There is a copy of this painting in Keats-Shelley Memorial House, Rome.

On long-term loan from Lord Abinger

[56] *Percy Bysshe Shelley (1792–1822)*

Epipsychidion

London: C. and J. Ollier, 1821

Epipsychidion was published anonymously in London in an edition of perhaps 200 to 250 copies. In sending the fair copy manuscript (now lost) to his publisher Charles Ollier, together with the 'Ode to Naples', Shelley wrote: 'The longer poem I desire should not be considered as my own; indeed, in a certain sense, it is a production of a part of me already dead. … It is to be published simply for the esoteric few … and it would give me no pleasure that the vulgar should read it.'

The American poet Robert Frost said that his reading of the poem changed his life by changing his idea of love. It is an attempt by Shelley to describe feelings of tenderness to three women in his life at one given moment. As he told his friend John Gisborne: 'if you are anxious, however, to hear what I am and have been, it will tell you something thereof. It is an idealized history of my life and feelings'. Shelley refers to his wife Mary as the moon, to Claire Clairmont as the comet, and to Teresa Viviani (called Emily in the poem) as the sun. For Shelley, Emily is much like Dante's Beatrice, real and ideal at the same time. In reality 'Emily' was the nineteen year-old daughter of the governor of Pisa, and was kept in the convent of St Anna while awaiting arrangements for her marriage. Shelley's final paeon in praise of Emily is a testament to the power of love; he creates in words an ideal setting (a Greek island) and an ideal relationship.

The title of the poem is derived from the Greek *epi*, meaning 'upon', and *psychidion*, meaning 'little soul'.

The Geoffrey Bindman Collection, purchased in 2004 with the support of the Heritage Lottery Fund, the J. Paul Getty Jr Charitable Trust, the Friends of the National Libraries, Sir Harry and Lady Djanogly, the Charles Warren Bequest, the Roger and Sarah Bancroft Charitable Trust, the Chris Brasher Trust, John and Sally Barker, John Dobson, and other private donors

EPIPSYCHIDION:

VERSES ADDRESSED TO THE NOBLE

AND UNFORTUNATE LADY

EMILIA V——

NOW IMPRISONED IN THE CONVENT OF ——

L' anima amante si slancia fuori del creato, e si crea nel infinito
un Mondo tutto per essa, diverso assai da questo oscuro e pauroso
baratro.   HER OWN WORDS.

LONDON

C AND J OLLIER VERE STREET BOND STREET

MDCCCXXI.

[57] *Percy Bysshe Shelley*

Adonais, An Elegy on the Death of John Keats

Pisa: 1821

John Keats died at Rome on 23 February 1821. Shelley, then living in Pisa, wrote to Claire Clairmont on 16 June 1821: 'I have received a most melancholy account of the last illness of poor Keats, which I will neither tell you nor send you; for it would make you too low-spirited. My elegy on him is finished: I have dipped my pen in consuming fire to chastise his destroyers; otherwise the tone of the poem is solemn & exulted.'

Shelley described the poem as 'a highly wrought *piece of art*', 'the least imperfect of my productions'; 'It is better than any thing that I have yet written', he told Claire Clairmont, '& worthy both of him & of me.' The poem concludes brilliantly with the awareness of his own vulnerability:

> my spirit's bark is driven,
> Far from the shore, far from the trembling throng
> Whose sails were never to the tempest given;
> The massy earth and sphered skies are riven!
> I am borne darkly, fearfully, afar;
> Whilst burning through the inmost veil of Heaven,
> The soul of Adonais, like a star,
> Beacons from the abode where the Eternal are.

Adonais was printed in Pisa under the poet's supervision, in an edition of probably less than a hundred; 'it is beautifully printed, & what is of more consequence, correctly' Shelley told his English publisher Charles Ollier. He instructed Ollier to have another edition printed in England, but the poem sold badly, and Ollier did no more than sell the initial copies, which remain scarce.

The Geoffrey Bindman Collection, purchased in 2004 with the support of the Heritage Lottery Fund, the J. Paul Getty Jr Charitable Trust, the Friends of the National Libraries, Sir Harry and Lady Djanogly, the Charles Warren Bequest, the Roger and Sarah Bancroft Charitable Trust, the Chris Brasher Trust, John and Sally Barker, John Dobson, and other private donors

ADONAIS

AN ELEGY ON THE DEATH OF JOHN KEATS,
AUTHOR OF ENDYMION, HYPERION ETC.

BY

PERCY. B. SHELLEY

Ἀστὴρ πρὶν μὲν ἔλαμπες ἐνι ζώοισιν ἑῶος.
Νῦν δὲ θανὼν, λάμπεις ἕσπερος ἐν φθίμενοις .

PLATO.

PISA

WITH THE TYPES OF DIDOT

MDCCCXXI.

[58] *Mary Shelley (1797–1851)*

Frankenstein: or The Modern Prometheus

London: Lacking, Hughes, Harding, Mayor & Jones, 1818

On the evening of 17 June 1816 the Shelleys were visiting Byron at the Villa Diodati by Lake Geneva. '[I]t proved a wet, uncongenial summer' Mary Shelley remembered, 'and incessant rain often confined us for days to the house. Some volumes of ghost stories, translated from the German into French, fell into our hands. … "We will each write a ghost story," said Byron; and his proposition was acceded to.' The result was a fragment by Byron (published in 1819 against his wishes with *Mazeppa*) on the theme of the vampire; a gothic novel by Byron's personal physician John Polidori, *Ernestus Berchtold, or The Modern Oedipus* (1819); and, most famously, Mary Shelley's first novel, *Frankenstein*, which was published, anonymously, in 1818. As befits a Gothic novel, which explores the approaches to the unconscious, it was inspired by a reverie. Mary Shelley wrote in 1831:

> I saw – with shut eyes but acute mental vision – I saw the pale student of unhallowed arts kneeling beside the thing he had put together. I saw the hideous phantasm of a man stretched out, and then, on the working of some powerful engine, show signs of life, and stir with an uneasy, half-vital motion. Frightful must it be; for supremely frightful, would the effect of any human endeavour to mock the stupendous mechanism of the Creator of the world. His success would terrify the artist; he would rush away from his odious handwork, horror-stricken. He would hope that, left to itself, the slight spark of life which he had communicated would fade …

Later scenes in the novel draw upon Mary Shelley's subsequent tour of the Alps with Shelley, most powerfully in the meeting between Frankenstein and the Creature on the Mer de Glace.

The Geoffrey Bindman Collection, purchased in 2004 with the support of the Heritage Lottery Fund, the J. Paul Getty Jr Charitable Trust, the Friends of the National Libraries, Sir Harry and Lady Djanogly, the Charles Warren Bequest, the Roger and Sarah Bancroft Charitable Trust, the Chris Brasher Trust, John and Sally Barker, John Dobson, and other private donors

FRANKENSTEIN;

OR,

THE MODERN PROMETHEUS.

IN THREE VOLUMES.

Did I request thee, Maker, from my clay
To mould me man? Did I solicit thee
From darkness to promote me?——
PARADISE LOST.

VOL. I.

London:

PRINTED FOR

LACKINGTON, HUGHES, HARDING, MAVOR, & JONES,
FINSBURY SQUARE.

1818.

[59] *Lord Byron (1788–1824)*

Portrait by Richard Westall (1765–1836)

1813   Oil on canvas, 91.8 × 71.1 cm

This one of the best-known images of the most celebrated, and most portrayed poet of the day. With his aristocratic demeanour, personal charm and beauty, he seemed the very image of what a poet should be. 'If you had seen Lord Byron, you could scarcely disbelieve him' wrote Coleridge in April 1816, 'so beautiful a countenance I scarcely ever saw – his teeth so many stationary smiles – his eyes the open portals of the sun – things of light, and for light – and his forehead so ample, and yet so flexible, passing from marble smoothness into a hundred wreathes and lines and dimples correspondent to the feelings and sentiments he is uttering'. Part of Byron's appeal was that he offered himself as a personality to the reader, first as the gloomy Childe Harold and then, more wittily, more outrageously, as the narrator of *Don Juan*. He knew and used the power of the image, icon almost, in both words and paint. His works sold.

The artist, Richard Westall, was better known for his book illustrations and watercolours, and was later commissioned by John Murray to provide a set of twenty-four illustrations for Byron's narrative poetry. Despite his objections, this portrait was endlessly copied and engraved, and the poet's already rather dreamy expression became increasingly romanticised. R.C. Dallas commented that 'the picture of Byron by Westall is superior to the others, but does not come up to the original. As for the copies and engravings which have been taken from these pictures and circulated, they are all exaggerated and deserve the appellation of caricatures.'

On long-term loan from the National Portrait Gallery, London

[60] *Lord Byron*

Hours of Idleness. A Series of Poems, Original and Translated

Newark: S. and J. Ridge, 1807

Byron's first collection of poetry, *Fugitive Pieces*, was printed privately in 1806, then quickly withdrawn and burned by the author after he received objections to its 'erotic' imagery. In March 1817 he wrote to William Bankes: 'Contrary to my former intention, I am now preparing a volume for the Public at large, my amatory pieces will be expunged, & others sub-situted, in their place; the whole will be considerably enlarged, & appear the latter end of May'. The result was his first published volume, *Hours of Idleness*.

In an ill-advised preface, Byron put himself forward as a youthful, mod-est, but high-ranking man of leisure: 'To produce any thing entirely new, in an age so fertile in rhyme, would be a Herculean task, as every subject has already been treated to its utmost extent. – Poetry, however, is not my primary vocation; to divert the dull moments of indisposition, or the mon-otony of a vacant hour, urged me "to this sin;" little can be expected from so unpromising a muse.' Seizing upon this preface (which was removed for the second edition) Henry Brougham (a Whig) gave the volume a scoffing notice in the *Edinburgh Review*: 'The poesy of this young Lord belongs to the class which neither Gods nor Men are said to permit.' Byron's response was to write the satirical poem *English Bards and Scotch Reviewers*. In 1821, on hearing of Keats's death in Rome (according to Shelley, a direct result of the devastating reviews of *Endymion*), Byron wrote to John Murray: 'I know, by experience, that a savage review is hemlock to a sucking author; and the one on me knocked me down – but I got up again. Instead of burst-ing a blood-vessel, I drank three bottles of claret, and began an answer ...'.

Oliver Turnbull Bequest, 2004

HOURS OF IDLENESS,

A

SERIES OF POEMS,

ORIGINAL

AND

TRANSLATED,

By GEORGE GORDON, LORD BYRON,

A MINOR.

Μητ' αρ με μαλ' αινεε μητε τι νεικει.
HOMER. Iliad, 10.

Virginibus puerisque Canto.
HORACE.

He whistled as he went for want of thought.
DRYDEN.

Newark:

Printed and sold by S. and J. RIDGE;
SOLD ALSO BY B. CROSBY AND CO. STATIONER'S COURT;
LONGMAN, HURST, REES, AND ORME, PATERNOSTER-
ROW; F. AND C. RIVINGTON, ST. PAUL'S CHURCH-
YARD; AND J. MAWMAN, IN THE POULTRY,
LONDON.

1807.

[61] *Thomas Love Peacock (1785–1866)*

Nightmare Abbey

London: T. Hookham Jun., 1818

Thomas Love Peacock was a novelist, essayist and poet who looked upon prominent Romantic figures, including his close friend Percy Bysshe Shelley, with a delightfully satiric eye. *Nightmare Abbey*, his third novel, is perhaps his finest work. Peacock wrote it while reading Canto IV of Byron's *Childe Harold*. 'The fourth canto of *Childe Harold* is really too bad', he wrote to Shelley, 'I cannot consent to be *auditor tantum* of this systematical "poisoning" of the "mind" of the "reading public"'. Byron in Peacock's novel is satirised as the gloomy Mr Cypress: 'Sir, I have quarrelled with my wife; and a man who has quarrelled with his wife is absolved from all duty to his country. I have written an ode to tell the people as much, and they may take it as they list.' Coleridge can be found in the morbid Mr Flosky, who 'plunged into the central opacity of Kantian metaphysics, and lay *perdu* several years in transcendental darkness', while the central character, Scythrop Glowry, is partly derived from the youthful Shelley:

> [Scythrop] now became troubled with the *passion for reforming the world.* … He passed whole mornings in gloomy reverie, stalking about the room in his nightcap, which he pulled over his eyes like a cowl, and folding his striped calico dressing gown about him like the mantle of a conspirator.

'I am delighted with Nightmare Abbey' Shelley wrote to Peacock from Italy. 'I think Scythrop a character admirably conceived & executed … I suppose the moral is contained in what Falstaff says *"For God's sake talk like a man of this world,"* and yet looking deeper into it, is not the misdirected enthusiasm of Scythrop what JC calls the salt of the earth?'

The Geoffrey Bindman Collection, purchased in 2004 with the support of the Heritage Lottery Fund, the J. Paul Getty Jr Charitable Trust, the Friends of the National Libraries, Sir Harry and Lady Djanogly, the Charles Warren Bequest, the Roger and Sarah Bancroft Charitable Trust, the Chris Brasher Trust, John and Sally Barker, John Dobson, and other private donors

NIGHTMARE ABBEY:

BY

THE AUTHOR OF HEADLONG HALL.

> There's a dark lantern of the spirit,
> Which none see by but those who bear it,
> That makes them in the dark see visions
> And hag themselves with apparitions,
> Find racks for their own minds, and vaunt
> Of their own misery and want.　　BUTLER.

LONDON:

PRINTED FOR T. HOOKHAM, JUN. OLD BOND-STREET;
AND BALDWIN, CRADOCK, AND JOY,
PATERNOSTER-ROW.

1818.

[62] *Leigh Hunt (1784–1859)*

Portrait by Benjamin Robert Haydon

*c.*1811   Oil on canvas, 60.8 × 50.2 cm

Leigh Hunt was a poet and critic, and from 1808 the editor of the radical periodical, the *Examiner*, which he founded with his brother John. He came to prominence in 1812 when, following an attack on the Prince Regent in the *Examiner*, he was tried and imprisoned for libel. He was visited in his cell by, among others, Charles Lamb and Byron, who thought him 'not exactly of the present age. He reminds me more of the Pym and Hampden times – much talent, great independence of spirit, and an austere, yet not repulsive, aspect … He is, perhaps, a little opinionated, as all men who are at the centre of circles … might be'. He was later a close friend of Shelley and Keats, whose early work he encouraged and promoted.

This portrait was made shortly after Hunt and Haydon first met in June 1811, an occasion Haydon recalled in his *Autobiography*: 'we began to talk, and he to hold forth, and I thought him, with his black bushy hair, black eyes, pale face, and "nose of taste," as fine a specimen of a London editor as could be imagined; assuming yet moderate, sarcastic yet genial, with a smattering of everything and mastery of nothing … The fearless honesty of his opinions, the unscrupulous sacrifice of his own interests, the unselfish perseverance of his attacks on all abuses, whether royal or religious, noble or democratic, ancient or modern, so gratified my mind, that I suffered this singular young man to gain … an ascendancy in my heart'. In 1816 Haydon told Hunt: 'do not forget that *your* Portrait is the only one I have painted or probably ever will.'

On long-term loan from the National Portrait Gallery, London

[63] *The Liberal. Verse and Prose from the South*

Issue One   London: John Hunt, 1822

The Liberal was jointly conceived in 1822 by Shelley and Byron in Pisa, and Leigh Hunt in England, who came to Italy to act as editor. Even as Hunt was arriving in Genoa, however, Shelley was confiding his doubts to Horace Smith: 'Between ourselves I greatly fear that this alliance will not succeed, for I, who could never have been regarded as more than the link of the two thunderbolts, cannot now consent to be even that – & how long the alliance between the wren & the eagle may continue I will not prophesy.' Following his death in July 1822 the project foundered, and only four issues appeared, between September 1822 and June 1823. Byron, who had been warned against the collaboration by friends such as Tom Moore, concluded: 'It was foolish of me to engage in it … for I have hurt myself without doing much good to those for whose benefit it was intended.'

The main contributors to *The Liberal* were Byron, Hunt and William Hazlitt. Two pieces by Shelley were included in the first issue: 'May-day Night; a Poetical Translation from Goëthe's Faust' and 'Song, written for an Indian Air'. The two greatest contributions were Byron's 'The Vision of Judgment', his attack on Robert Southey, which opened Issue One, and Hazlitt's essay 'My First Acquaintance with Poets', in Issue Three, an account of his first meetings in 1798 with Coleridge and Wordsworth, all three then in the spring of their careers.

The Geoffrey Bindman Collection, purchased in 2004 with the support of the Heritage Lottery Fund, the J. Paul Getty Jr Charitable Trust, the Friends of the National Libraries, Sir Harry and Lady Djanogly, the Charles Warren Bequest, the Roger and Sarah Bancroft Charitable Trust, the Chris Brasher Trust, John and Sally Barker, John Dobson, and other private donors

THE
LIBERAL.

VERSE AND PROSE FROM THE SOUTH.

TO BE CONTINUED OCCASIONALLY.

Nº I.

LONDON, 1822:

PRINTED BY AND FOR JOHN HUNT,
22, OLD BOND STREET.

PRICE FIVE SHILLINGS.

[64] *Benjamin West seated and talking to John Opie and Benjamin Robert Haydon*

Portrait by Thomas Stothard (1755–1834)

Inscribed on paper in brown ink and pasted on to the frame: 'Portraits of Benjamin West P.R.A. / Benjamin Robert Haydon / John Opie R.A.' Inscribed in graphite on the back of the oil painting: 'By T. Stothard / left to right / Benjamin West 1738-1820 / John Opie 1861–1807 / B.R. Haydon 1780–1846' Oil on board, 13.4 × 11 cm

If its inscriptions are to be believed, then this is an interesting oddity. Stothard's group portrait was presumably done from memory, with the intention of showing Haydon with his predecessors or rivals in historical painting and theory, or, perhaps, to imagine him elevated to the ranks of the Academicians. West, President of the Academy until 1821, was the most celebrated historical painter of his generation and although Haydon was highly critical of his work, his most important pictures were conceived in clear competition with it. Opie's *Gil Blas* was one of the few pictures that struck Haydon in the first Academy exhibition he saw in 1804. He called on Opie at the outset of his Academy studies, to see 'a clean gallery of masculine and broadly painted pictures' and to receive the good advice to ignore Northcote's disparagement of his studies of anatomy – '"He doesn't know it himself, and would be very glad to keep you as ignorant"' – and a not very subtle hint that he become his pupil. Haydon went with Wilkie to Opie's funeral in 1807, and later, in his *Autobiography*, mused on his decline from 'the wonderful Cornish boy – the gifted genius' to 'a disappointed man'. He had liked him, and his wife Amelia. Of his works he wrote, 'His lectures are admirable. Of the three, Fuseli, Opie and Reynolds, Opie came nearest to the Greek principles of form, led by his natural sagacity and shrewdness'.

Purchased 1996, with the support of Lord Egremont

154

STOTHARD

[65] *Benjamin Robert Haydon (1786–1846)*

Letter to William Wordsworth

31 December 1816   Manuscript

In November 1816 the twenty-one year-old John Keats wrote a sonnet celebrating three 'great spirits': Benjamin Robert Haydon, Leigh Hunt and William Wordsworth. Haydon promised to send the sonnet to Wordsworth, which he does in this letter:

> I copy out a Sonnet by a Young Poet Keats addressed to me, but beginning with you—I should wish very much to know what you think of it—he promises a great deal—and said in a letter to me when I promised to enclose it to you—"The idea of your sending it to Wordsworth puts me out of breath, you know with what Reverence I should send my well wishes to him." &c—

> Great spirits now on Earth are sojourning;
> He of the Cloud, the Cataract, the Lake,
> Who on Helvellyn's summit, wide awake,
> Catches his freshness from Archangel's wing:
> He of the rose, the violet, the spring,
> The social smile, the chain for Freedom's sake:
> And lo!—whose stedfastness would never take
> A meaner sound than Raphael's whispering.
> And other spirits there are standing apart
> Upon the forehead of the age to come.
> These, these will give the world another heart,
> And other pulses. Hear ye not the hum
> Of mighty workings?——
> Listen awhile ye nations, and be dumb.

Soon afterwards Keats sent the elder poet a copy of his 1817 *Poems* inscribed: 'To W. Wordsworth with the author's sincere reverence.'

Gordon Graham Wordsworth Bequest, 1935

Dec. 31. 1816

Dear Sir / I should have sent you by this Magazine [?] the first Print that has ever been engraved from any work of mine — it is only a head, but very finely translated [?] it in a study from a [?] and attracted some attention last Year — had it been of sufficient consequence I should with your leave have dedicated it to you — but this pleasure I reserve for the [?] first large Print from [?] my more important work. I hope [?] the frame maker could not get it ready, [?] must defer till next month —— I copy out a Sonnet by a [?] Poet, he at [?] beginning [?] addressed to me, but [?] he [?] you. I should wish very much to know you [?] think of — he promises a great deal — and said in a letter to me when I promised to enclose it to you — the idea of your sending it to Wordsworth puts me out of breath, [?] send me [?] what Reverence I should send my well wishes to him "[?]

Great Spirits now on Earth are [?]
He of the cloud the Cataract he [?]

[66] *John Keats (1795–1821)*

Lifemask by Benjamin Robert Haydon

1816   White plaster cast, 22 × 17 × 14 cm

Keats's lifemask was made by Benjamin Robert Haydon in 1816, in prepara-
tion for Keats's inclusion in his huge painting *Christ's Triumphal Entry into
Jerusalem* (together with the heads of Wordsworth, Voltaire, Isaac Newton
and William Hazlitt). 'You may now look at Minerva's Ægis with impu-
nity' Keats wrote to Cowden Clarke on 17 December 1816, shortly after it
was made, 'seeing that my awful Visage did not turn you into a John Doree
you may have accordingly a legitimate title to a Copy—I will use my interest to procure it for you.' Fanny Keats said the mask was 'a perfect copy of
the features of my dear brother. The expression of course is wanting as the
eyes are closed, and perhaps the mouth is a little compressed which is but
natural, as the mask could not have been taken with the lips unclosed. It is
perfect, except for the mouth, the lips being rather thicker and somewhat
compressed which renders the expression more severe than the sweet and
mild original'. In Haydon's painting Keats's mouth is indeed open, as if
talking animatedly to his friend, the artist William Bewick, who was then
one of Haydon's pupils.

   This copy of the lifemask belonged first to the Shelleys' son Percy
Florence Shelley, who gave it to Robert Louis Stevenson, who later took it
with him to Samoa, his last home.

Gift of Dallas Pratt, 1993

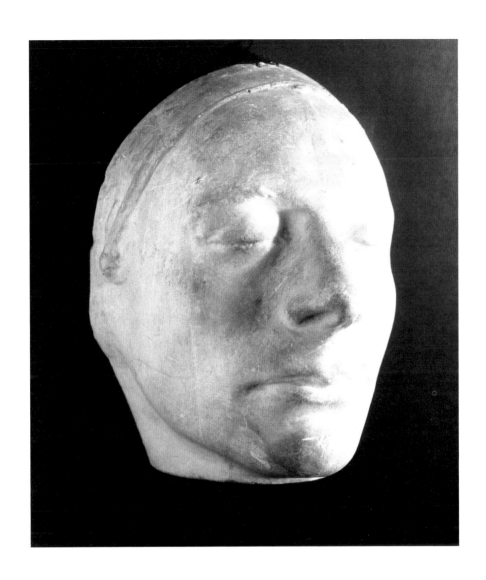

[67] *John Keats*

Poems

London: C. and J. Ollier, 1817

Keats published this, his first volume of poetry, in 1817. It contained one great sonnet, 'On first looking into Chapman's Homer', a host of minor sonnets and verse epistles, his first known poem, 'Imitation of Spenser', and the two long poems, 'I stood tip-toe on a little hill' and 'Sleep and Poetry'.

Among Keats's immediate circle the book was received with celebration. 'I have read your Sleep and Poetry' Haydon told him, 'it is a flash of lightening that will sound men from their occupations and keep them trembling for the crash of thunder that *will* follow.' Among the world at large, however, it made little, if any impact. Charles Cowden Clarke recalled: 'The first volume of Keats's minor muse was launched amid the cheers and fond anticipations of all his circle. Every one of us expected (and not unreasonably) that it would create a sensation in the literary world; for such a first production (and a considerable portion of it from a minor) has rarely occurred . . . Alas! the book might have emerged in Timbuctoo with far stronger chance of fame and approbation.' It was scarcely reviewed outside Keats's circle (although the sonnet and particularly the dedication to Leigh Hunt were fuel for the hostile reviews of the later *Endymion*) and the first edition remained unsold for many years. As Keats himself wrote in his original, unpublished preface to *Endymion*: 'About a twelvemonth since, I published a little book of verses; it was read by some dozen of my friends, who lik'd it; and some dozen who I was unacquainted with, who did not. Now when a dozen human beings are at words with another dozen, it becomes a matter of anxiety to side with one's friends;—more especially when excited thereto by a great love of Poetry.'

The Geoffrey Bindman Collection, purchased in 2004 with the support of the Heritage Lottery Fund, the J. Paul Getty Jr Charitable Trust, the Friends of the National Libraries, Sir Harry and Lady Djanogly, the Charles Warren Bequest, the Roger and Sarah Bancroft Charitable Trust, the Chris Brasher Trust, John and Sally Barker, John Dobson, and other private donors

𝔓𝔬𝔢𝔪𝔰,

BY

JOHN KEATS.

" What more felicity can fall to creature,
" Than to enjoy delight with liberty."

Fate of the Butterfly.—SPENSER.

LONDON:

PRINTED FOR

C. & J. OLLIER, 3, WELBECK STREET,

CAVENDISH SQUARE.

1817.

[68]   *John Keats*

Lamia, Isabella, the Eve of St Agnes and other Poems

London: Taylor and Hessey, 1820

By April 1820, Taylor had the completed manuscripts for a new volume of Keats's poetry; 'Next week Keats's new Volume of Poems will be published', he wrote to his father on 26 June, '& if it does not sell well, I think nothing will ever sell again.' To Hessey he wrote three days later: 'The Book looks every thing that I could wish, & at 7/6 is cheap in my opinion'. Keats however was less confident: 'My book is coming out with very low hopes, though not spirits on my part', he had written to Charles Brown earlier that month, 'This will be my last trial; not succeeding, I shall try what I can do in the Apothecary line.'

    Lamia, Isabella, The Eve of St. Agnes and other Poems was published at the beginning of July. It contained many of the poems for which Keats is now famous: the odes ('To Psyche', 'To a Nightingale', 'On a Grecian Urn', 'On Melancholy', 'To Autumn'), 'Lamia', 'Isabella', 'Hyperion', 'The Eve of St Agnes'. There were a number of favourable notices. Writing in the *New Times*, Charles Lamb picked out 'Isabella' and 'The Eve of St Agnes' for particular praise, writing of the latter: 'like the radiance, which comes from those old windows upon the limbs and garments of the damsel, is the almost Chaucer-like painting, with which this poet illumines every subject he touches. We have scarcely anything like it in modern description.' 'My book has had a good success among literary people,' Keats wrote in August, 'and, I believe, has a moderate sale.' Taylor, however, was still advertising the first edition eight years later.

Gift of Simon Nowell-Smith, 1985

LAMIA,

ISABELLA,

THE EVE OF ST. AGNES,

AND

OTHER POEMS.

BY JOHN KEATS,

AUTHOR OF ENDYMION.

LONDON:

PRINTED FOR TAYLOR AND HESSEY,

FLEET-STREET.

1820.

[69] *J.M.W. Turner (1775–1851)*

A View of Menaggio, Lake Como

1842–3   Pencil and watercolour, 18.8 × 27.2 cm

Wordsworth first saw Como on his 1790 walking tour of the Alps with Robert Jones. He wrote to Dorothy:

> The lake is narrow and the shadows of the mountains were early thrown across it. It was beautiful to watch them travelling up the sides of the hills for several hours, to remark one half of a village covered with shade, and the other bright with the strongest sunshine. ... The shores of the lake consist of steeps covered with large sweeping woods of chestnut spotted with villages, some clinging from the summits of the advancing rocks, and others hiding themselves within their recesses. Nor was the surface of the lake less interesting than its shores; part of it glowing with the richest green and gold the reflexion of the illuminated woods and part shaded with a soft blue tint. The picture was still further diversified by the number of sails which stole lazily by us, as we paused in the woods above them. After all this we had the moon. It was impossible not to contrast that repose that complacency of Spirit, produced by these lovely scenes, with the sensations I had experienced two or three days before, in passing the Alps.

Wordsworth, along with Mary and Dorothy, visited Como again during his tour of the Continent in 1820. They lodged at Menaggio, shown in this late watercolour by J.M.W. Turner.

Gift of Charles Warren, 1997

[70] *Charlotte, Emily and Anne Brontë*

Poems by Currer, Ellis and Acton Bell

London: Smith, Elder & Co., 1846

The idea that she and her sisters could jointly publish a volume of poetry came to Charlotte Brontë when she came upon some of Emily's poems: 'One day, in the autumn of 1845, I accidentally lighted on a MS volume of verse in my sister Emily's handwriting. Of course, I was not surprised, knowing that she could and did write verse; I looked it over, and something more than surprise seized me, – a deep conviction that these were not common effusions, nor at all like the poetry women generally write. I thought them condensed and terse, vigorous and genuine. To my ear, they had also a peculiar music – wild, melancholy and elevating.'

It was quickly decided that the sisters should use masculine pseudonyms: 'we did not like to declare ourselves women', Charlotte remembered, 'because – without at that time suspecting that our mode of writing and thinking was not what is called "feminine" – we had a vague impression that authoresses are liable to be looked on with prejudice.'

A thousand copies of this volume were originally printed, at the Brontës' own expense, and the first copies arrived at Haworth in May 1846. Sales were almost non-existent. In June 1848 Charlotte Brontë wrote: 'In the space of a year, our publisher has disposed of but two copies … Before transferring the edition to the trunkmaker, we have decided on distributing as presents a few copies of what we cannot sell'. She sent copies to Wordsworth, Thomas De Quincey, Hartley Coleridge and Tennyson. In November 1848 961 remaining copies were transferred to Smith, Elder & Co., who re-issued the book with a cancel title page, retaining the original date, as here. Very few copies of the first issue have survived.

Oliver Turnbull Bequest, 2004

POEMS

BY

CURRER, ELLIS, AND ACTON

BELL.

LONDON:

SMITH, ELDER AND CO., 65, CORNHILL.

1846.

THE DISCOVERY OF THE LAKE DISTRICT

Jean-Baptiste Claude Chatelin & François Simon Ravenet after William Bellers

'A View of Derwentwater, Towards Borrodale.'

London: Boydell and Sayer, 17 January 1774
Engraving and etching, 40 × 54.1 cm

The first published depictions of the Lake District were by William Bellers and Thomas Smith [see no. 72]. Bellers' view of Derwentwater was issued in London in 1752, engraved by the fashionable French artists Chatelin and Ravenet. The composition is classically arranged according to the manner of seventeenth century Italian and French landscape painting, while the elegant foreground figures, added by Louis-Philippe Boitard, seem to identify the area with the leisured classes in the south. A Claudean light bathes the whole scene. The view across the lake towards the entrance to Borrowdale was probably taken from Castle Head, a rocky hillock rising up from the valley floor near the Keswick road. Geologically, the hill is a volcanic plug.

In 1754 this print was included as part of the set *Six Select Views in the North of England*, together with views of Windermere, Haweswater, Ullswater, Derwentwater from Vicar's Island, and Bywell Bay in Northumberland. This set was republished in 1757 with the addition of three other prints in a collection entitled *Nine Views of the Lakes in the North of England*. The original six prints were finally reprinted by John Boydell in 1774 with the addition of two other prints, in a collection entitled *Eight Views of the Lakes in Cumberland*. When in the late eighteenth century William Gilpin, the inventor of the picturesque tour, declared that the earliest artists depicted the Lake District mountains as if they were haycocks, it seems that he had the works of Bellers in mind.

Purchased 1986

[72] *Thomas Smith (d. 1767)*

A View of Darwentwater &c. from Crow-Park

London: John Boydell, 1767
Line engraving, 38.3 × 55 cm

Originally published by the artist in 1761 as a set of three (with views of Thirlmere and Windermere) entitled, *Three Views in the North of England*. They were republished by Boydell in 1767 together with a fourth view, of Ennerdale (showing Pillar Rock). An eight-page pamphlet, now very scarce, accompanied the prints, entitled: *A Short Historical Account of Four Views in the North of England. With some cursorary [sic] Observations on the adjacent Country*.

The stumps of trees in the foreground memorialize the great stand of oak trees that were sold and cut down by the absentee landlords, the trustees of Greenwich Hospital, granted the confiscated estates of the Jacobite earls of Derwentwater. This axing of the trees was a cause of lamentation among men of taste; 'If one single tree had remained, this would have been an unparallel'd spot', wrote Thomas Gray, 'and Smith judged right, when he took his print of the Lake from hence, for it is a gentle eminence, not too high, on the very margin of the water, and commanding it from end to end, looking full into the gorge of Borrowdale'.

Smith was the father of the artist and mezzotint engraver John Raphael Smith (1752–1812). His view of Derwentwater is more subtle in mood than that by Bellers, attempting to evoke some of the contrasting propeties of 'beauty, horror and immensity' remarked upon by John Dalton and John Brown. The distant fells of Borrowdale, greatly emphasised and partly shrouded by an approaching storm, appear dark and threatening; but the corn stooked on the island and harvested in the boat, together with the cattle in the water, suggest fertitlity and plenty.

Purchased 1986

[73] *Lady Mary Lowther (1739–1829)*

'Winander-Mere, the Long Island, Bonus, Rayrigg's &c &c, a Peep of the Sea of Milthorp & Lancaster with the Castle, from the Top of Orrost'

1767   Watercolour, 32.5 × 56.5 cm

This drawing was originally attributed to Coplestone Warre Bampfylde (1719–1791), a distinguished amateur draughtsman, but further research has suggested that he was not the artist. A series of sketches, including the first draft for this picture, can be found in a handmade sketchbook that belonged to Lady Mary Lowther, the daughter of the Prime Minister Lord Bute, and the neglected wife of Sir James Lowther.

The scene from Orrest Head coincides with Wordsworth's view of landscape as described in *The Prelude*: he speaks of liking to view the sea 'laughing in the distance'. The artist here is trying to present as much of the panorama, including the sea, as she can manage. Lancaster Castle, seen across Morecambe Bay, was nearly thirty miles distant. The farmhouse on the island of Windermere was soon to be replaced by the round classical tower designed by John Plaw in 1775. Plaw exhibited his designs as a 'fantasia' for Lake Windermere at the Royal Academy in that year. But clearly the owner of the island, Thomas English, and his successors the Christian / Curwens, felt Plaw's classical design was more in keeping with their perception of the Lake District as a northern Arcadia.

Before the Round House was built, critics such as William Hutchinson in his *Excursion to the Lakes* (1776), had attacked Mr English for building garden walls about the farmhouse, which Hutchinson claimed spoiled the beauty of the island. Claife Heights, bare of trees, is shown as Wordsworth would have first known it before the great planting in about 1790 of oaks and larches by John Christian Curwen and Richard Watson, Bishop of Llandaff.

Purchased 1986, with the support of the MGC/V&A Purchase Grant Fund

[74] *Lady Mary Lowther*

'Part of Ulls Water, a distant View of Kirkstone Paterdale, the
Church & Hall, St Sundays Craggs, Stybury Craggs, Glen Redding
Pykes Glen Coyen, Birch Fell, from Govery High Park'

1767   Watercolour, 32.5 × 56.5 cm

Mary Lowther's panoramic drawing is taken from, and shows part of,
Govery High Park, better known as Gowborrow Park, the area on the west-
ern shore of Ullswater to the south of which Wordsworth and his sister
Dorothy first saw the 'dancing' daffodils on 15 April 1802.

   This drawing is the source of Francesco Zuccarelli's oil painting (done
in Italy) which formerly hung at Lowther Castle. This large picture (6 feet
by 10 feet) seems remarkable in that Zuccarelli had misunderstood Lady
Mary's drawing (or felt that the theme needed enlivening) for he took the
liberty of introducing rapids into the middle of Ullswater. His foreground
has exotic Italian peasants, and some majestic cattle and goats (a species
present on the hills near Patterdale at the end of the eighteenth century).
The whereabouts of the Zuccarelli oil is at present unknown.

Purchased 1986, with the support of the MGC/V&A Purchase Grant Fund

[75] *Joseph Farington (1747–1821)*

View towards Latrigg

Dated 17 October 1775   Watercolour, 37.3 × 58.8 cm

Joseph Farington was the son of the Vicar of Leigh, Lancashire. He studied with Richard Wilson at the Royal Academy. From 1775 he became fascinated with the Lake District and he made it his purpose to illustrate every view mentioned by Thomas Gray in his 'Tour of the Lakes', 1769, first published by William Mason in York in March 1775 (as a part of *Life and Letters of Thomas Gray*). This, the earliest of Farington's Lake District sketches, is dated October 1775, which indicates how faithfully he wished to observe the actual places, in the very same month (October) when Gray himself had visited in 1769. Gray's own account of 1769 reads: 'Passed by the side of Skiddaw and its cub called Latrigg; and saw from an eminence, at two miles distant the vale of Elysium in all its verdure; the sun then playing on the bosom of the Lake; and lighting up the mountains with its lustre.'

   Farington takes his view from Crow Park, his back towards the lake, the houses of Keswick in the middle distance.

Purchased 1994, from the collection of Ian Fleming-Willliams

[76] *Joseph Farington*

Grasmere

Dated 14 June 1777   Pencil, pen and wash, 32 × 47.2 cm

In 1777 and 1778 Joseph Farington toured the Lakes with Sir George Beaumont and Thomas Hearne. This is the earliest known drawing of Grasmere. Farington's viewpoint is taken from Dunmail Raise, and undoubtedly
he chose it because it is substantially the viewpoint of Thomas Gray's
description in his letter of October 1769. Note the marvellous subtlety in
Farington's technique – the different tints of grey, lightening in the distance;
the pen in the foreground being thick, and in the distance thin.

   When Farington did this drawing he had not had the benefit of reading
Thomas West's *Guide to the Lakes*, first published 1778. West criticised Gray
for describing Grasmere from Dunmail Raise rather than from the Red
Bank approach, whereby the lake is in the foreground and Dunmail Raise
in the distance. For his later engraving of Grasmere, one of the twenty
Views of the Lakes published in a folio volume in 1789, Farington's choice
of viewpoint is from Penny Rock, at the southeast corner, rather than Red
Bank, at the southwest. This was to become the classic view of Grasmere.
These views from the south, with Helm Crag a central pyramid, were to
become the classic image of Grasmere.

Purchased 1984, with the support of the Victoria & Albert Museum Purchase Grant Fund

[77] *Joseph Farington*

Lodore Waterfall, Westmoreland

1785   Pen and ink, watercolour, 29.8 × 33 cm

This is one of Farington's exhibition watercolours of the Lake District. He did not complete this ambitious series until 1790, and most of it is now to be found in a bound volume of some thirty drawings at the Mellon Centre at Yale.

Farington's first success at the Royal Academy was his painting of the Lower Falls at Rydal (1781). Thereafter he proceeded to publish *Twenty Views of the Lakes,* which began to appear in parts in 1783 and was completed in 1789. The letter press was written by Wordsworth's influential uncle, and Farington's friend, William Cookson. Cookson was a Fellow of St John's College Cambridge, and became one of the Royal tutors and a Canon of Windsor. Dorothy Wordsworth was to spend more than five years in his household.

Among the *Twenty Views* is an engraving entitled 'Lowdore Waterfall, from Brandelow Woods' (15 April 1785): the plate was engraved by W. Byrne and T. Medland. This watercolour is a fresh articulation of this subject and shows a nearer view of Lodore than that found in the print.

Gift of the W.W. Spooner Charitable Trust, 2004

Thomas Hearne (1744–1817)

Sir George Beaumont and Joseph Farington painting a Waterfall

1777   Pen and wash, 41 × 28.5 cm

It is possible that in these drawings Hearne is alluding to Claude's land-scape, *Morning*, where the artist can be seen under the shade of an umbrella painting 'an antique temple' outside Rome. The purpose of the umbrella is not only to keep the surface dry and clean, but most of all to keep the light evenly spread on the artist's canvas. It is absolutely clear that the artists are painting in oils out of doors. The more approved method was that the artist would first draw in pencil or charcoal, and then work up the picture through watercolour to the oil. Increasingly in the Romantic period, the watercolour itself, with its sense of spontaneity, became the prized artistic work.

The scene here is Lodore Falls on the south-east shore of Derwent-water. The artists draw, or paint, their English scene intently, as if at work on a classic subject such as the falls at Tivoli, near Rome. There is a draw-ing of this waterfall by Beaumont in the Tate Gallery.

Purchased 1984 from the Beaumont family, with the support of the National Heritage Memorial Fund and the Victoria & Albert Museum Purchase Grant Fund

[79] *Thomas Hearne*

The West Aspect of Furness Abbey, Cumbria

Dated 6 August 1777   Watercolour, 18.8 × 26.7 cm

Between 1777 and 1781 Thomas Hearne was engaged in the production of
a series of drawings and engravings which would make up *The Antiquities
of Great Britain* collection. This is one of a number of sketches of Furness
Abbey. It is concerned with architectural detail, and yet absorbs the poetic
pastoral scene: everywhere, the skilful use of the pen emphasises the softness of the vegetation, while Hearne ingeniously makes use of the vertical
lines of the laid paper to help with the depiction of the columns and piping
around the windows and doorways. Hearne took pains to invest his topographical drawings with effects of light and atmosphere seldom attempted
by previous draftsmen in watercolour.

In Book II of *The Prelude* Wordsworth writes how he and his schoolboy
companions would often recklessly ride to the abbey (the distance was
strictly too far for the hired horses); and movingly describes the song of a
wren that he hears there:

> ... from the roofless walls
> The shuddering ivy dripped large drops, yet still
> So sweetly 'mid the gloom the invisible bird
> Sang to itself that there I could have made
> My dwelling-place, and lived for ever there
> To hear such music.

The mood of calm that the ruins and the birdsong evoked for Wordsworth
are perhaps never closer to being captured than in Hearne's picture.

*Purchased 2003, with the support of the National Art Collections Fund, the Beecroft Bequest
administered by the Museums Association, and the W.W. Spooner Charitable Trust*

[80] *Paul Sandby (1730–1809)*

Keswick Lake

*c.*1780 Gouache, 14 × 23.3 cm

Paul Sandby, a teacher of drawing for military purposes, is the earliest master among English watercolourists who made use both of transparent watercolours and of body colour, exemplified here. The latter's opaqueness gives the picture a solidity, and at the same time allows the artist to present brilliant and assertive details. Crosthwaite Church can be seen immediately below Skiddaw; and Joseph Pocklington's Island is crowned with his new house, an eighteenth-century 'white box', which he completed in 1779. A few houses straggle beneath Skiddaw, with the small hill of Latrigg to the right-hand side of the picture. A mass of houses, representing Keswick, is just discernible.

On the right-hand side of the drawing the surface has been scuffed, perhaps because, as the crease-mark suggests, the drawing had once been folded over and kept in an album.

Purchased 1991, with the support of the MGC/V&A Purchase Grant Fund

Thomas Gainsborough (1727–1788)

Langdale Pikes

1783   Pencil and wash, 26.7 × 41.7 cm

It is probable that Gainsborough travelled to the Lakes with the painter De Loutherbourg in August 1783. There are only three known drawings from Gainsborough's single tour of the Lakes, all of them drawn very freely with the brush, and clearly made on the spot. Langdale Pikes is an atypical attempt at topographical accuracy: as Constable noted of another Gains-borough work, 'With particulars he had nothing to do, his object was to deliver a fine sentiment …'. It is a tribute to his inquisitiveness that late in age he should undertake the difficult journey of nearly 300 miles to view this region, admired by Gray and painted by such serious artists as Wright of Derby, Paul Sandby, De Loutherbourg and Thomas Hearne.

The picture shows a figure standing in a rowing-boat in the foreground; Elterwater stretches across the foreground and middle distance; the hill to the left is Lingmoor; the Langdale Pikes dominate in the distance.

Gift of Charles Warren, 1985

[82] *John Bernard Gilpin (1701–1776)*

Rocky Pool

Pen and wash, 38.3 × 27.9 cm

One of an album of forty drawings by John Bernard Gilpin, a Carlisle drawing master, the father of William Gilpin, and a member of a large artistic
and literary circle.

Unlike his son, the exponent of the picturesque, the father, a one-time
topographer for the military, took fewer liberties with his actual landscapes.
His favourite subjects are either mountainous rocky scenes, often with
waterfalls or streams, or ideal landscapes where the rugged forcefulness
is replaced by an atmosphere of quiet and repose, and the influence of
Alexander Cozens is evident. The album also contains a view of Tyrim
castle on Loch Moydart, 'from a drawing by Mr. Paul Sandby'. Occasionally
the artist uses watercolour, but his usual method is to finish the drawings
with a series of grey washes. His pupils included, besides his sons William
and Sawrey, John 'Warwick' Smith.

*Purchased 1992, with the support of the MGC/V&A Purchase Grant Fund and the National Art
Collections Fund*

William Gilpin (1724–1804)

Ideal Scene

*c.*1786   Pen & wash, 16.6 × 23.6 cm

William Gilpin was the son of John Bernard Gilpin. He was a clergyman and schoolmaster, who in his spare time wrote books on 'Picturesque Beauty', not only on the Lake District, but also on the Wye Valley in Wales and on the Highlands of Scotland. His popularity grew because he made travelling entertaining; he encouraged searching for fine landscapes which would be suitable either for an amateur to draw, or for a tourist to admire with his eye. The books were known to Wordsworth even as an undergraduate, and the reason is perhaps that he was at school with Gilpin's nephew, Charles Farish, and, further, had been brought up in the Lake District which was increasingly the subject of commentary from connoisseurs such as Thomas Gray, Thomas West and Gilpin himself.

Gilpin's concern was to find the 'picture' in the landscape, and thus train one's eye to look at landscape as if one were a painter. It was obviously not necessary to paint oneself to take pleasure in the 'picture' that the eye had found. The oval drawings represented here were Gilpin's usual method of illustrating his books. The first artist he used to produce these aquatints was John 'Warwick' Smith, an artist also born in Cumbria and, indeed, trained by Gilpin's father. Gilpin thought of his drawings as improvements on what the eye saw – indeed, he suggested that there was no need to draw the Lake District accurately since Joseph Farington had already done it. Here, on the right, he adds a round tower. It is Gilpin's peculiar skill to be able to design his drawings with an acute sense of shade and subtle colouring, and an intimate suggestibility about the shapes – perhaps buildings or perhaps trees-makes his scenes interesting.

Purchased 1992, with the generous help of the V&A Purchase Grant Fund and the National Art Collections Fund

[84] *John 'Warwick' Smith (1749–1831)*

Windermere

1788–92   Watercolour 35 × 52 cm

John 'Warwick' Smith was a pupil of John Bernard Gilpin, and was the first to provide the oval aquatint prints, admired for their skill in presenting shade and tone, in William Gilpin's publications. But Smith was plucked away when Lord Warwick, meeting him at a drawing party and seeing his skill, offered to send him to Italy. There, between 1776 and 1781, he famously met William Pars, Thomas Jones, John Robert Cozens and finally Francis Towne; with whom he returned from Italy.

This is one of more than a hundred watercolours drawn as part of a portfolio of views of the English Lake District, all commissioned by John Christian Curwen, of Workington Hall and of Belle Isle on Lake Windermere, and executed between 1788 and 1792. It is typical of John 'Warwick' Smith to make a portfolio of drawings. It is not until 1805, when the Watercolour Society puts on its earliest exhibitions that he made it a habit to put his work on public display. Up to that point it had been his custom to draw a series of studies for a particular patron.

Curiously, his absence from public exhibitions seems to have built up his reputation among his fellow artists. They, and the general public, were conscious of his work through his publication of prints of his work (scenes of Italy, 1794, and of the English Lakes, 1795 and 1796). Amongst his admirers was Julius Caesar Ibbetson who admired Smith's capacity to draw 'the tint of air'. It is this element, which involves catching elements of the weather, that is one of Smith's distinctive qualities. In this particular drawing of Lake Windermere with clouds he presents a dramatic view of mountains to the west of the Lake rising above the mist that is emerging from the surface of the lake. The Langdale Pikes and Loughrigg show at the right hand side. This is a scene of quiet drama, not least because the clouds, somewhat unexpectedly, are below the mountain tops.

Purchased 2002, with the support of the National Art Collections Fund, the Beecroft Bequest administered by the Museums Association, and the W.W. Spooner Charitable Trust

[85] *John 'Warwick' Smith*

The Upper End of Coniston Lake, Cumbria

Dated 1801   Pencil and watercolour, 34.3 × 50.8 cm

This picture shows the northern end of Lake Coniston. The low building on the shore no longer exists; but it was formerly the inn at Coniston
Waterhead, destroyed in the first part of the nineteenth century. Pictures of
the inn are rare. Its removal appears to be part of the dandifying of the lake
carried out by the Knott family, who possessed the house formerly called
Coniston Waterhead, and now renamed Monk Coniston.

    The drawing is a good example of Smith's work. As usual, there is the
interest in Smith's handling of colour, which to his fellow artists was a
source of envy. It is not Smith's practice to use ink as an outline (as with his
friend Towne) but as here, to carefully draw in pencil, which is not easily
detectable. Here also, Smith has not used any monochrome wash – the
local colour is painted direct onto the paper. The shadows are obtained
by putting an extra wash of the pure colour. The 'tint of air' that Smith
catches in his drawing is the wind, blowing south through the tree, but
eddying northwards on the surface of the lake.

*Purchased 1990, with the support of the MGC/V&A Purchase Grant Fund and the National Art
Collections Fund*

[86] *Francis Towne (1740–1816)*

Elterwater, Cumberland

Dated 1786   Pen and ink, watercolour, 23.6 × 37.4 cm

Towne came to the Lake District in August 1786, where for a little over two weeks he worked tirelessly and made a large number of drawings. Basing himself in Ambleside, he explored that area thoroughly. Towne made his sketches 'on the spot'; he had two notebooks. Rather than make separate finished works from these sketches, he would then, over time, colour them, separate them from the notebooks, and finally mount and inscribe them. A collection of the drawings was exhibited in a one-man exhibition in 1805. In thus staying true to his original vision, Towne's drawings have an individuality and distinctiveness that separates them from work done consciously within the formal traditions of Lake District scenery. His concentration on a particular area was also individual; he evidently preferred catching the same place under differing light and weather conditions to travelling around and sketching from Thomas West's recommended viewing stations.

Nothing better illustrates Towne's great sense of an ordered universe than this drawing, with each section of the hill, Lingmoor, slotting into its sculpted place, like a three-dimensional jigsaw. The Langdales to the right, towering above Elterwater, are nevertheless given no dramatic presence. They are made part of an elegant harmony, and the whole image is bound together by the great 'Z' of water that flows into the foreground. The house, Elterwater Hall, gives a sense of scale.

Purchased 1982, with the support of Cecil and Ann Parkinson

[87] *Francis Towne*

'A Valley in the Lake District'

Dated 4 September, 1786   Pen and ink, watercolour, 23.2 × 37.5 cm

This is one of the large drawings which were the product of Towne's visit to the Lakes in 1786, and possibly one of three views of Rydal that he exhibited nearly twenty years later in 1805.

Many of the 1786 drawings were in the sketchbooks, and deliberately crossed over the central fold, thus emphasizing the panoramic stretch of the scene, but 'A Valley in the Lake District' is a drawing on a larger sheet which allows Towne to present a surprising amount of detail. Interestingly, it seems to involve him in drawing from more than one viewpoint. On the left, his view includes Loughrigg, the glacially ravaged hill which runs from the south side of Rydal Water and Grasmere. The right hand side of the drawing is dominated by Silver How, which marks the western shore of Grasmere. On the right hand side, in the middle distance, Towne shows the road which travels from White Moss quarry over to Dove Cottage, the very road that Wordsworth and his sister Dorothy travelled when they came to live in Grasmere in 1799. In the near foreground are the bays and promontories that make up the shoreline when seen from the north bank of the River Rothay as the water leaves the east end of Rydal lake. The road over White Moss cannot be seen today, so it is possible that Towne added the detail by examining the view from the southern bank of the river.

Despite such puzzles, Towne's drawing generally suggests topographical accuracies. In the centre of the design, there is a small white building, in fact a barn, still standing today. Towne perhaps enlarges the building, but as usual in his work, such a structure gives scale to the whole scene.

Purchased 2002, with the support of the Resource/V&A Purchase Grant Fund, the National Art Collections Fund, Sir Harry and Lady Djanogly, and the W.W. Spooner Charitable Trust

[88] *John White Abbott (1763–1851)*

Grasmere, Helm Crag

Dated 12 July 1812   Watercolour, 19 × 29.5 cm

John White Abbot was a pupil of Francis Towne, a fellow Devonian. He was an assiduous and dedicated follower of Towne's method, as can be seen from the drawing of Grasmere, made in 1791 during his long tour of Scotland and the Lake District, and one of his earliest drawings to survive. It appears to have originally formed part of a sketchbook, and in its clarity and distinctive colouring clearly shows Towne's influence.

Abbott's viewpoint eliminates the island completely (interestingly, Gray was blamed by West for not mentioning the island as a feature of the landscape). Dunmail Raise, the pass to the north, is represented by an exquisite low curve with the hill, Seat Sandal, to the right. The church is placed underneath Helm Crag; it acts at once as a measuring rod and, at the same time, as a marker of the religious importance of the place. Grasmere, if paradisal, was also of the matter-of-fact world of all of us.

Purchased 1977, with the support of the National Art Collections Fund

[89]   *John Laporte (1761–1839)*

Vale of Keswick from Ashness Bridge

c.1800   Watercolour and bodycolour, 46.8 × 65.1 cm

Laporte was a distinguished drawing master. From 1806 he held the post of Professor of Drawing at Addiscombe Military Academy, and among his pupils there was Dr Thomas Monro (1759–1833), the connoiseur and collector whose circle included Sandby, Rooker, Hearne, Gainsborough, Wilson, Cozens, and the young Girtin and Turner. Laporte made his first tour of the Lake District in 1790, and the area remained a favourite subject; between 1797 and 1833 he exhibited a total of twenty-four Lake District scenes. In 1792 a series of engravings after his Lake scenes was published by T. Gowler. This drawing is on a large scale, and is painted in a combination of bodycolour and watercolour. Though not listed in the catalogues of either the Royal Academy or the British Institution, it is clearly intended as an exhibition piece. The composition is directly influenced by Farington's engraving of 1784.

Wordsworth recommended Ashness Bridge as affording a 'fine bird's-eye view'. Laporte shows Skiddaw on the right, and many of the well-known buildings of the area, including Crosthwaite Church, and the house and fort on Vicar's Island, built by the island's owner Joseph Pocklington between 1778 and 1781. In the distance he appears to show Ormathwaite, the home of Dr. William Brownrigg, one of the most famous Cumbrians of his time. Laporte visited Ormathwaite in the early 1790s, when the house seems to have become the meeting place for younger artists. An amateur artist, Joseph Wilkinson, was a resident of Ormathwaite, and was influenced by Laporte's use of bodycolour in his own drawings for *Northern Scenery*, 1795. Eight works by Laporte, six of them using bodycolour, are listed among the pictures catalogued for sale when Wilkinson left for Norfolk in 1804.

Gift of the W.W. Spooner Charitable Trust, 2000

[90] *James Gillray (1757–1815)*

Mary of Buttermere

1800   Pencil, pen and ink, 26.8 × 20.5 cm

This drawing of the beautiful Mary Robinson was apparently taken from life in 1800 and adapted into a print when the scandal of her bigamous marriage to James Hatfield broke in October–November 1802, largely through articles sent by Coleridge to the *Morning Post*. Drawings by James Gillray are extremely rare, for he had the ability to draw directly onto the plate, and to write in reverse form. He was quite willing to use sketches by other people, but he had a decided preference for using the actual appearance of a figure, whether in caricatured or non-caricatured form.

In a print derived from this drawing and considerably less complimentary to the Beauty of Buttermere, Gillray has put at the bottom of his print 'del.t & fec.t' indicating that the sketch was his own, and the print was his also. The surprising thing is that he has also put 'Sketch'd From Life, July 1800'. This suggests that Gillray had made a visit to the Lake District in 1800, a fact not otherwise known.

This drawing was purchased along with an unpublished letter dated 11 November 1802 from Coleridge to Colonel Moore; in this the poet interestingly mentions 'Mrs Hatfield', with great concern and sympathy, and her bigamous husband as a kind of nightmare figure: 'he engrosses my waking Thoughts, he disturbs my Sleep—I can scarcely keep my Tongue from cursing him, hourly.'

Purchased 1993, with the support of the MGC/V&A Purchase Grant Fund, the National Heritage Memorial Fund, the National Art Collections Fund, the Binks Trust, the Clark Trust, Jared Curtis, Kenneth Ewing, John Harding, Kenneth Harris, Frank Herrmann, Mary Lovell, the Sir George Martin Charitable Trust, Robert Pirie, Peter Placito, Tom Stoppard, Oliver Turnbull and Delia Twamley

[91] *Edward Dayes (1763–1804)*

Keswick Lake and Skiddaw

1791   Pen, blue and grey wash, 27.6 × 38.7 cm

Edward Dayes had ambitions as an historical painter, but depended on topographical drawing and teaching to make a living. Thomas Girtin was one of his pupils. He had a horror of excess and roughness, and sought to produce a balanced and harmonious effect in his landscapes. 'One effect should, as much as possible, be calculated to excite painful, the other agreeable sensations', he wrote in the 'Essays on Painting' (published in *The Works of the Late Edward Dayes*, 1805), 'Mountains involved in clouds, and objects seen through a mist, will always appear with more dignity than if distinctly viewed … all agreeable sensations are founded in temperance: too great a quantity of light, color, or sound, excites pain'.

The view is taken from Barrow Common. Pocklington's house can be seen on the island. The figure appears to be raised up, his legs apparently dangling over the cliff edge; as the figure looks to the view, so his dog looks at the artist. The rough, vigorous foreground contrasts with the more exquisite distant view, which gains formality through the shadowy reflections of Skiddaw in the lake. Dayes has a characteristic manner of catching the play of light on the landscape, giving a notion of its clarity by a brilliant definition of detail on the background hills.

Gift of Charles Warren, 1985

Thomas Girtin (1775–1802)

Borrowdale

*c.*1801   Pencil and watercolour, 31 × 47.1 cm

Thomas Girtin, for a time a pupil of Edward Dayes, seems never to have visited Cumbria, but he still executed a number of Lake District landscapes. This drawing of Borrowdale is derived from an earlier sketch by Sir George Beaumont. The two artists knew each other by 1799, when Beaumont became an associate member of Girtin's Sketching Club, an evening drawing society in London. Girtin took and developed a number of Beaumont's sketches, including versions of Watendlath and Culloth Force, and Beaumont, despite his strong preference for oil painting, owned and treasured several of Girtin's watercolours, including this one of Borrowdale.

Girtin has energized Beaumont's sketch in various ways – for instance, he has suggested an aperture in the rocks through which the horizontal lines of the plain below can be seen. It is those very lines to the right-hand side which make the valley seem to have an increased distance when compared to Beaumont's drawing (below). This is a trick Girtin learned from imitating Cozens when he and Turner sat together on the same bench making drawings for Dr Monro, Turner and Girtin then being only seventeen years old. Girtin's lines can often be identified by the morse code effect they seem to give. He has also given the mountain in the background an extra shoulder which moves forward as if about to embrace the whole scene. The cloud across it, again, enhances the grandeur, giving a sense of height.

Purchased 1986 from the Beaumont family, with the support of the National Heritage Memorial Fund, the National Art Collections Fund, and the MGC/V&A Purchase Grant Fund

[93] *John Constable (1776–1837)*

Langdale Pikes from Elterwater

Dated 4 September 1806   Pencil, 23.6 × 37.4 cm

John Constable was brought up in the flat country of East Anglia, to the
north-east of London. He made one memorable visit to the Lake country
in 1806. Since England was at war with France, it was impossible to visit
the Alps, as many of his predecessors had done. The Lake District provided Constable with the most varied mountain scenery, which, despite
the dreadful weather, he drew passionately and inquisitively; some ninety
drawings were produced in less than two months. Mysteriously, the great
finished oils which we know he exhibited have now disappeared.

On the back of the picture is a label by Charles Golding Constable, the
artist's son: 'This view in the English lake district was taken by my father,
John Constable r.a. when he was thirty years of age. The date on the sketch
is in Constable's own handwriting. C.G. Constable'. This would make
the drawing one of Constable's earliest explorations of the mountainous
scenery to the west of Lake Windermere. He seems to use his pencil, with
its vigorous right-hand swing, as a weapon to sculpt out the surface of the
panoramic landscape.

*Purchased 1985, with the support of the MGC/V&A Purchase Grant Fund, Provincial
Insurance, the Francis C. Scott Charitable Trust and other private donors*

[94] *John Constable (1776–1837)*

Helvellyn

Dated 21 September [1806]   Watercolour, 19.4 × 36.2 cm

Constable had come to the Lake District a rather depressed young man who had yet to establish himself as an artist of promise. The landscape of this northern region must have been liberating for him. Here were few human figures (usually none); homesteads appear as ghostly outlines; fields have little cultivation. The relative freedom from man in the Lake District allowed Constable to paint other things – rough plants, weather, waterfalls. Hills were walked up as well as seen from a distance, and shown with a new sense of their structure, their organic architecture. Constable's fame came at the end of his life, when he became a friend of Wordsworth and showed, like the poet, the need to record the grandeur of the green world of nature as a setting where the working man, with his boats, his horses, his harvesting, had an appropriate place.

Though there is an inked inscription, 'Helvellyn in Cumberland', that shows through from the verso and is in Constable's hand, this drawing seems little faded; the blue and green washes rarely survive.

Purchased 1985, with the support of the MGC/V&A Purchase Grant Fund, Provincial Insurance, the Francis C. Scott Charitable Trust and other private donors

[95] *William Green (1760–1823)*

Grasmere

1802   Watercolour, 13.8 × 20.1 cm

As a seventeen-year-old Manchester surveyor's assistant, Green was involved in 1778 in a survey of Lancashire. At Ulverston he met Thomas West, who encouraged him to become an artist. He visited the Lakes several times between 1791 and 1794, and began publishing aquatints of the district in 1795. In 1800 he settled in Ambleside and devoted his considerable energies to recording the scenery and buildings and to providing large numbers of engravings which tourists could take away with them.

Green's enormous number of prints, the most ambitious series of the area since Farington, were carried out in aquatint or soft-ground etching, expertly engraved and published by himself, assisted in the colouring by his daughters. He opened Exhibition and Sale Rooms at Ambleside and Keswick where he exhibited and sold his work. His views, which were painstakingly accurate, have left us a remarkable and detailed record of mountains, lakes, rocks, trees and particularly buildings. Green was on good terms with Wordsworth. He is buried in the churchyard at Grasmere, and Wordsworth recorded in the inscription: 'twenty-three years … passed in this neighbourhood where, by his skill and industry as an artist he reproduced faithful representations of this country and lasting memorials of its more perishable features'.

The deciduous woods to the left were shortly to be felled, to the dismay of the Wordsworths, for they had been a favourite walking place, and the setting for Wordsworth's poem 'Point Rash Judgment' (1800). The mountain is Loughrigg, and the horizontal path, Loughrigg Terrace, is visible. The two figures in the boat in the centre of the picture are shown with fishing rods. This was a common pursuit of both Wordsworth and his sailor brother John.

Purchased 1992, with the support of the MGC/V&A Purchase Grant Fund

[96] *William Havell (1782–1857)*

Waterfall at Ambleside, seen through a window

1807   Watercolour, 32.3 × 26 cm

It was John Glover's success with exhibiting watercolours of subjects from the Lake District in the 1806 and 1807 exhibitions of the Society for the Painters of Watercolours, that prompted Havell to go with Reinagle to Ambleside. Havell stayed at least twelve months, knew the Hardens of Brathay, and was known to Wordsworth, who, somewhat warily, asked his friend Beaumont what he thought of Havell's work: 'When you have seen Havill's drawing of Rydale pray tell me what you think of it. I have not much confidence in my judgment of Pictures except when it coincides with yours'. Beaumont indicated that Havell and all his watercolourist friends, through neglecting the art of painting in oils, were on the wrong tack: 'this was the very error of the French—they're always ingenious and always wrong'. Beaumont told Wordsworth: 'if you can inspire him with a little humility you will be of great service to him & facilitate his progress'.

Beaumont had been further irritated by Havell when he heard him praising Turner as a colourist at the expense of the admired seventeenth-century landscape painter Claude Lorrain.

Purchased 1990, with the support of the MGC/V&A Purchase Grant Fund

[97] *Thomas Rowlandson (1756–1827)*

Doctor Syntax Sketching the Lake

*c.*1812   Watercolour, 11 × 19 cm

The Tour of Doctor Syntax, a series of aquatints by Thomas Rowlandson with verse commentary by William Combe (1741–1823) was published by Ackermann in 1812. The illustrations and verses had originally appeared under the title 'The Schoolmaster's Tour' in monthly editions of the *Poetical Magazine* between 1809 and 1811. Doctor Syntax, an elderly clergyman and schoolmaster, and self-styled artist, poet pand musician, travels the country having various mishaps. Where Rowlandson's drawings satirise the vogue for travel in general, Combe's text targets the picturesque in particular, and his character bears considerable resemblance to William Gilpin. This illustration shows Syntax sketching a lake on which a group of tourists are boating; his horse, Grizzle, drinks from the lake and a puzzled fisherman looks on. It was accompanied by the following lines:

> Soon as the morn began to break
> Old Grizzle bore him to the lake;
> Along the banks he gravely pac'd,
> And all its various beauties trac'd.
> But Grizzle, in her haste to pass,
> Lur'd by a tempting tuft of grass,
> A luckless step now chanc'd to take,
> And sous'd the Doctor in the lake.

Rowlandson draws in reverse so that the image is the opposite way round when printed from the copperplate.

Purchased 1992, with the support of the MGC/V&A Purchase Grant Fund and the National Art Collections Fund

[98]   *George Fennel Robson (1788–1833)*

Grasmere

*c.*1830   Watercolour, 42.7 × 81.5 cm

Robson's presentation of Grasmere reveals a fresh eye. Seat Sandal, rather than Helm Crag (centre left) is the dominant fell in the scene, and Stone Arthur is placed above the church. Grasmere is made glamorous and spectacular. Note that the central house in the picture is Wordsworth's former home at Allan Bank (where he lived from 1808 to 1811). Robson has the image of the cows in the water, a motif that was used by Thomas Smith in 1761 to depict the sense of warmth and plenty, and would be used again in Victorian painting and photography. In the twenty-first century cattle have virtually disappeared from Grasmere where sheep now dominate. This has changed the texture of the hills' surfaces; the spread of bracken is now a problem. The presence of cattle meant that the bracken on the fells grew less strongly, since their feet bruised the fronds and, further, bracken was cut to provide bedding (it was also curtailed by being cut, dried and then burnt to produce alkali for the making of soap).

Purchased 1983, with the support of the Victoria & Albert Museum Purchase Grant Fund and the National Art Collections Fund

99

Edward Lear (1812–1888)

Grasmere

Dated 5 October 1836   Pencil and watercolour, 16.8 × 25.4 cm

This is one of eight Lake District drawings by Edward Lear owned by the Trust and formerly in the possession of his godchild, who emigrated to New Zealand. There are known to be at least twenty-eight such drawings in total, and they are Lear's first major effort at landscape. Hitherto, most of his work had been close studies of birds, and rare animals kept in zoos. In these early works he revealed considerable graphic skill and a command of gorgeous colour.

In 1836 he made a visit to the Howards of Levens Hall, near Kendal, and from there made several excursions to the heart of the Lake District. The first landscapes are tentative though capable drawings, made in July 1836 of Windermere and of Coniston; but in September and October 1836 a new daring and confidence comes into his treatment of mountains and lakes. What is more, the drawings have an exquisite accuracy in their topography. Here, he shows the Red Bank road, newly engineered, and so suitable for carriages.

Purchased 2004, with the support of the National Art Collections Fund and the W.W. Spooner Charitable Trust

100

James Baker Pyne (1800–70)

Windermere from Orrest Head

Dated 1849   Oil on canvas, 82 × 132 cm

This painting deals imaginatively with a landscape which had been at the heart of a vital controversy throughout the previous six years. The picture shows two trains – one in the station and the second leaving Windermere for Kendal and Oxenholme. Wordsworth had led a campaign against the building of the railway to the Lake District; he succeeded in that he prevented its being built any further than Windermere: all the plans for taking it through to Ambleside, Grasmere and on to Keswick had to be abandoned.

Wordsworth's position is easily misunderstood. He was not against railways as such but simply believed that to bring railways to the heart of the Lake District would also bring people who would demand the pleasures of the town: his view was that the Lake District was a sort of 'national property that belonged to whoever had an eye to perceive or the heart to enjoy'. Despite Wordsworth's sonnets and letters to the *Morning Post*, and a great deal of correspondence, the Windermere railway was finally opened in 1847; the chairman of the company was Cornelius Nicholson, a young man whom Wordsworth had known since his boyhood in Ambleside. Their relationship survived this conflict. Pyne's picture is a wonderful celebration of the new railway line: we see the scene from an aerial view from Orrest Head. The reality of travelling by train from Windermere is described by Thomas Carlyle who declared that the horror of travelling from the Lakes to London was: 'nine hours of tempestuous, deafening nightmare – like hours of Jonah in the whale's belly'.

It is interesting to note the differences between this painting and the early drawing by Lady Mary Lowther [no. 73] taken from a similar but higher position on Orrest Head.

Purchased 2000, with the support of the Resource/V&A Purchase Grant Fund, the National Art Collections Fund, the Chris Brasher Trust, and Lord and Lady Chorley

Rural Regeneration
Cumbria

northwest
development agency

INVESTING IN
englands**northwest**